M. N. GOLOVI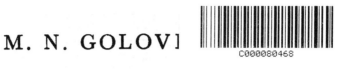

*

Conflict in Space

A Pattern of War in a New Dimension

*

ST MARTIN'S PRESS

NEW YORK

Acknowledgments

I wish to express my gratitude to:

Mr. Thurstan James for reading the typescript and suggesting improvements;

General P. Gallois for his very clear definition of certain aspects of deterrent strategy, with particular reference to *credibility factors* (Chapter I);

Messrs. T. Rudenski and B. Featherstone for checking some of the numerical material and drawing the graphs and diagrams;

My wife and Miss B. Merchant for preparing the typescript for print.

THE AUTHOR

To

H. BURROUGHES

F.R.Ae.S.

Preface to the American Edition

While the present book was written by a European for Europeans and most of the technical information presented will be familiar to American readers, the concept of *Attrition in Space* applied to world politics and strategy may be a somewhat novel and controversial hypothesis.

As stated in the original Preface, data included in the book were valid up to October, 1961, when the English edition went to print. Later events have drawn attention to military astronautics, but—broadly speaking—these developments did not affect the main structure of the present essay.

Nevertheless it might be of interest to point out five items which—directly or indirectly—tend to confirm the basic thesis of *Conflict in Space*:

1. Colonel J. Glenn's orbital flight on 20th February and Commander Scott Carpenter's on 24th May, 1962, provided *incontrovertible* evidence that manned vehicles can orbit the Earth for a limited period of time at comparatively low altitudes without environmental ill-effects upon their crews.

2. Early in 1962 the USAF outlined their new Space Plan defining a number of targets over a period of ten years. This plan was presented to the House Armed Services Committee in the form of a report by Lt.-Gen. J. Ferguson.

3. The US Government's decision to tighten up security in military astronautics, with particular reference to launches of specialised orbitals, indicates that certain types of satellite systems are now considered to be in the "vulnerable information" area. Incidentally, it has been suggested that the non-identification of launches was dictated by defence considerations, as a precaution against possible interception by hostile devices.

4. Mr. Khrushchev's recent announcement that the USSR now had a missile which could strike at the US Heartland from an unprotected direction suggests that the Soviets may be considering either a missile with a programmed trajectory, or else some form of simplified orbital weapon. The latter device, armed with a nuclear warhead of over 100 megaton yield and designed to explode in a low orbit, fits in with the theory that *incendiary satellites* could be used on a strategic scale. Incidentally, according to the Soviet newspaper *Red Star*, by 1970 the main weapon in the USSR aerospace arsenal will be a nuclear-armed satellite.

A conceivable *cold-war* episode might be country "A" putting into orbit a heavy long-life satellite, accompanied by "press leaks" to the effect that the payload is a multi-megaton bomb. The rumour may or may not be confirmed officially, according to Government "A" 's policy at the time.

To prevent a possible accident due, say, to the malfunction of the electronic circuitry, country "A" would use a dummy warhead or no warhead at all. Thus, unless the hostile satellite can be "interrogated", there would be no means of ascertaining whether it is a genuine threat or merely a military exercise with a simulated weapon.

It is highly improbable that country "B" would retaliate by firing surface-based strategic missiles thus starting a major nuclear conflict. The only reasonable defensive measure would be the launching of an anti-satellite device to destroy or neutralise the "un-cooperative object" in orbit.

Naturally such a display would cause an uproar, but for reasons of military prestige country "A" may well decide to run the risk of ensuing political unpleasantness. The real question is what useful action can be taken by country "B" without adequate defensive space armament?

5. In view of the un-cooperative attitude of the USSR at the Geneva Disarmament talks, the USA are fully justified in conducting a further series of nuclear tests. As reported in the press, these experiments will include explosions in the ionosphere and, possibly, at orbital heights.

While all nuclear tests can be regarded as reprehensible, it is difficult to see how the USA can work out a reliable pattern of aerospace defence without determining the degree of effectiveness of atomic counter-weapons against the warheads of ballistic missiles and, eventually, of orbital devices. It has been suggested that the recent Soviet nuclear tests did provide some very valuable information and that Marshal Malinovsky's claim to have perfected an anti-ICBM defence system may be based on the results of these trials.

Finally, the increase of US space budgets foreseen in Chapter IV (pages 79 and 80) has now been confirmed. It would appear that the NASA Fiscal Year 1963 grand total of research, development, construction and operation funds will be in the region of $3.8 billion, plus the $1.5 billion Department of Defence contribution directly connected with military astronautics.

London—May, 1962

Contents

Chapter III *Growth of Aerospace Technology*   37

Ballistic weapons, "building blocks" of new aerospace systems · US ballistic missiles and first orbital · Five generations of space vehicles and devices · Payloads and schedule of future launchings · Soviet ballistic missiles and reported space programme

Chapter IV *Industry and Budgets*   61

Post-World-War-I and Post-World-War-II aircraft industries · Diversification and expansion: electronics, propellants, ground support equipment · Pattern of aerospace industry, preponderant role of major concerns · Research and "forward thinking" · USA budgets and costs of aerospace systems · Situation in Western Europe, governmental action towards a joint programme · Possible scale of expenditure and participation of Western European industry · Estimated USSR budgets

Chapter V *Further Evolution of Aerospace Weapons*   87

Importance of aerospace weapons, contrast in Western European and US military thinking · Main categories of US projects · Subdivision into offensive, defensive, ancillary and logistic systems · Offensive weapons: boost-gliders and bombardment satellites · Defensive weapons: barrage, anti-satellite orbitals and anti-ICBM devices · Ancillary, supporting and logistic systems · Manned spaceflight, lunar vehicles and further developments · Payload costs

Chapter VI *Aerospace in World Politics and Strategy*   110

Increasing importance of aerospace in Grand Strategy · Ballistic "Deterrent-in-Being" and orbital "Deterrent-in-Action" · Attempts to evade conventional deterrent deadlock · Attrition in space and first combat in orbit · Orbital war and eventual aerospace supremacy of one of the opponents · Resolution of world conflict in space · Role of non-participating nations · Possible world hegemony of Power victorious in aerospace

CONTENTS

Plates

——————

Introduction

―――――

It must be made clear that the present study is not intended as a prophecy of future events in the realm of Power Politics and Grand Strategy—in fact the reader is invited to treat the contents of this book simply as a broad analysis and extrapolation of an existing situation. Moreover, the extrapolation is of a hypothetical nature: for instance, one of the postulates is that no global war will occur—by accident or design—say, in the course of the current decade. While the present state of tension could well lead to a world-wide catastrophe, it is to be hoped that the potential opponents will be wise enough to refrain from political gambling prompted by an unrealistic assessment of risks involved. By now the competing Powers must have realized the disparity between costs and returns of an atomic world conflict—in other words the very high probability of both victor and vanquished emerging in a state of utter devastation, having suffered casualties running into millions of human lives.

The second hypothesis is that while a major calamity will be avoided, West and East eventually will be forced into a trial of strength to resolve their differences. Modern science and technology applied to weapon design and construction opens a new field of warfare, which, oddly enough, may enable the contestants to achieve a solution by the force of arms without causing incalculable damage on the surface of the Earth.

It has been said that the history of mankind is the history of war. Even a superficial study of recorded events will show that there was a number of military or technical *breakthroughs*—for example, the emergence of new tactical concepts, often combined with the use of new weapons—which gave a temporary advantage to one of the opponents. It must have happened when bow and arrow were invented; nearer to us in time the Homeric warrior, protected by his bronze helmet and armour, could easily overcome a more primitively-armed enemy.

The growth of civilized communities—such as the Greek City States—was reflected in the appearance of more orderly military formations. With the passage of time great leaders and better-organized States were able to put in the field large and well-trained units exemplified by the Macedonian phalanx and the Roman legion. So long as the morale of the fighters remained unimpaired and the quality of the troops did not deteriorate due to the influx of low-grade mercenaries, hoplites and legionaries were virtually invincible.

The medieval knight was the precursor of the armoured fighting vehicle. The tactical designation *lance* emphasized the idea of an integrated unit, consisting of the knight supported by his squires and personal attendants. This was a distinct improvement on the disorderly hordes of barbarians surging all over Europe after the military and political collapse of the Western Roman Empire.

The next major breakthrough was the invention of gunpowder, which happened to coincide with the emergence of solidly-organized mercenary troops—the Swiss foot and the German *Landsknechten*. Eventually the knight's supremacy was terminated by the rise of communities aware of their unity of race or interests; thus, the central cantons of Switzerland, trading cities in the Netherlands, the Hanseatic League, Venice and Genoa could challenge the might of the feudal armies.

Further innovations came in rapid succession—the rifled barrel, ironclads, improved mobility, etc. Early in the twentieth century the aeroplane made its appearance; it began its career as an ancillary arm, but towards the end of the First World War fighters and bombers could no longer be regarded merely as "tactical nuisances".

Finally, in World War II no major operation could be attempted without air supremacy—or at least some measure of local air superiority.

Now, beyond the intermediate phase of ballistic missiles, a

new system of weapons is discernible—the truly three-dimensional aerospace devices and vehicles.

The reader might be interested to know the meaning and derivation of the term *aerospace*. The following definitions apply to the present study:

AERONAUTICS: the science and technology of locomotion in the atmosphere.

ASTRONAUTICS: the science and technology of locomotion outside the terrestrial atmosphere.

The definitions are simple and clear, but they do not cover the intermediate types of vehicles and devices circulating on the outer fringes of the atmosphere. Even at heights of several hundred miles traces of air are still present and the word astronautics is not strictly applicable; therefore, the term *aerospace* will be used to indicate the region where aerodynamics and ballistics interact or closely succeed each other as parts of a combined pattern.

The vehicles and devices which will constitute future three-dimensional weapon systems will operate in the vicinity of the Earth—at least for a few decades to come. Aerospace is the proper term to use, but in some special instances it may be preferable to talk of *orbital space*. The two designations are in a certain sense synonymous, but the latter is more definite, particularly in the case of current military projects. On the other hand, new derivations such as *aerospace industry* are now accepted in technical literature; the word *orbital* is much more limiting and cannot be used to convey the same meaning.

*

The technical sections of the present book are founded almost entirely upon US thinking and practice. The explanation of such an apparent bias is simple: the American Press provides a great deal of data, while Soviet communiqués give only a very limited amount of information. Work done in other countries—though quite interesting in itself—is in a different class, far below the level achieved in USA and USSR.

All information embodied in the text is unclassified, derived solely from the technical Press. If, in the course of evaluation and discussion the writer may have touched upon matters in "restricted areas", all deductions are purely coincidental and clearly within reach of any technically-minded person interested in the subject under review.

Finally, the contents of this book reflect the author's personal views and opinions only and have no connection whatsoever with any of the organizations or societies to which he may belong in his professional capacity.

CHAPTER I

Evolution of Grand Strategy

Clausewitz's definition of war as the continuation of politics by other means remains valid, but modern warfare has now become a very intricate process and the strategic planning and control of operations calls for an unprecedented input of thought and study. There can be a number of definitions of the word *strategy*: fundamentally, strategy deals with battles as a means of winning a war, while tactics is the art and science of winning battles. In the present context the term Grand Strategy will be used to indicate concepts, ideas and methods applicable to military operations on a global scale.

In practice Grand Strategy is an expression of national aspirations and ideological urges. Since Power Politics cannot be conducted effectively without the threat or even the use of armed force, Grand Strategy must form an integral part of political action on a world scale.

The present chapter will be devoted to the study of the existing situation and of factors contributing to the continuation of the present state of tension. The picture is complicated by the fact that, in addition to national interests and aspirations, ideological motives and impulses exert a considerable influence upon the general psychological environment. Thus, political doctrines of the Communist and Hitlerite type sharpen the aggressiveness of hidden nationalist aims. The primeval urge to aggrandize the tribe, community or nation originates conflicts which are rendered more acute by ideological fanaticism fostered by irresponsible leaders. The intervention of the

I

ideological stimulus is very dangerous in one particular aspect: it creates a pattern of irrational behaviour on the part of whole nations and events may be triggered off without the benefit of restraining thought. Thus, it becomes possible for a community or nation to engage in a conflict which to any sane individual would obviously be suicidal.

The Spanish Civil War of 1936–39 was a small-scale conflict of the "semi-emotional" type. A purely internal affair degenerated into a hidden international contest with pronounced ideological overtones, in the course of which the more realistically-minded military staffs found opportunities to try out new ideas and weapons.

The war of 1939–45—as distinct from World War I—was to some extent ideological. German leaders used the Nazi philosophy to stiffen the will of their people to fight and the fanaticism thus generated was very reminiscent of the Middle Ages. Historians will have a difficult task in disentangling the real and hidden motives of this particular war, but the results must be painfully obvious even to an uninformed observer. Instead of resolving an ideological conflict, World War II created a new state of tension where the place of German Nazism was taken by the aggressive expansionism of USSR and China.

As a result, the world entered upon a new phase of struggle for supremacy. This era began in 1945, immediately after World War II and ever since political tension has been fluctuating, Cold War episodes alternating with calculated attempts at "peaceful co-existence". These variations should be regarded as part of a single process of two major blocks striving for ideological and political survival or supremacy.

Differences in manpower resources, industrial potential and political maturity led to a regrading of the various Powers participating in the struggle. By reason of sheer numbers and of natural wealth concentrated within self-contained geographical areas, USA and USSR have emerged as the leaders of the two opposing camps.

In certain respects the present situation is reminiscent of

2

1939. A clash of opposing ideologies conceals the inner historical and economic mechanism which raises the intensity of the conflict to the level of a struggle for survival.

Various new techniques such as the *brainwashing* practised by the Chinese in the course of the Korean War give a foretaste of the psychological climate of an eventual World War III. This is far removed from the "polite" European wars of the nineteenth century and a better comparison would be the religious massacres of the Middle Ages. By contrast, Mongolian invasions were simple migrations of tribes driven by pressure of overpopulation and resulting shortages of food and grazing grounds.

The state of permanent conflict has found a tangible expression in the deterrent armament race; on a different plane, *visible* events assumed the form of peripheral wars and major incidents of the Berlin Blockade variety.

The most typical visible event of the last decade was the Korean War. This, in a way, was a trial of strength, but the opposing camps were not prepared to let the conflict grow into a world-wide conflagration. It is to be expected that further incidents will arise; for example, the Soviet offensive against the American Continent being clearly discernible as the background of the current troubles in Cuba. No doubt the USSR and her satellites will also show increased activity in S.E. Asia and in Africa; for instance, the confused state of affairs in Laos and the former Belgian Congo offers excellent opportunities for creating world-wide disturbances.

The current trial of strength is the Berlin crisis; this unfortunate inheritance of World War II, reminiscent of the "Danzig Corridor", presents both sides with a thorny problem which could involve considerable loss of political prestige. It is to be hoped that further exercises in "nuclear brinkmanship" will not lead to disaster; in the final analysis an atomic conflict on a USA-Western Europe-USSR scale can be profitable only to Mao Tse Tung's China.

While peripheral wars and incidents of all kinds cannot resolve the fundamental West-East conflict, small-scale operations will maintain tension and might well have an adverse effect on the economic stability of certain Western European nations. It is unlikely, however, that peripheral pressure alone could seriously affect the military posture of USA.

*

To analyse the present situation it is necessary to have a clear idea of the political and strategic struggle between the "Big U" Powers; this can be subdivided into four distinct periods or phases:

PHASE 1: immediately after World War II USA had a decisive superiority over USSR. American bombers could attack Soviet territory, while the Russians could only retaliate against USA's Western European allies. The US political status was unchallengeable and American forces could intervene to defend their allies without any risk of retaliatory action against their homeland: the long-range Red bomber formations were weak and had no atomic weapons which could represent a major threat to USA.

PHASE 2: the Soviets began to build up their nuclear armaments and a strategic force of bombers such as *Bears* and *Bisons*. Nevertheless, the Americans retained their air superiority, both in attack and in defence, the latter being sufficiently well developed to pose a very difficult problem to any potential enemy intending to reach targets in the US "Heartland". In a major conflict USSR had little chance of victorious survival and, as a result, could not openly challenge USA and had to resort to Cold War tactics.

PHASE 3: this is the present stage of the conflict which opened when strategic bombers began to lose their effectiveness, partly due to the appearance in service of new guided missiles and ground-controlled supersonic fighters. The parallel development of ballistic weapons altered some of the fundamental aspects of the deterrent theory, which became actively concerned with survival capabilities of the retaliatory ballistic armament.

The current state of affairs is further complicated by the

4

fact that the Soviets are supposed to have a certain degree of superiority in intercontinental ballistic weapons. Therefore, US intervention in European affairs or action on a global scale, as the result of some Cold War incident, will tend to become less certain. While in Phases 1 and 2 the US homeland was reasonably safe from reprisals, in the present situation any drastic action by the American Government would expose the whole country to the danger of a major atomic attack. Therefore, the *credibility* of nuclear US intervention in the event of limited aggressive action against European NATO countries is now somewhat diminished, resulting in a significant downgrading of the US deterrent as a deciding factor in Western Europe defence strategy.

The *credibility factor* [1] is a succinct way of expressing the probability of one or both opponents using strategic nuclear weapons and thus initiating a world conflict. It is very difficult to express this coefficient quantitatively, but Fig. 1 (overleaf) illustrates the idea in *qualitative* form. Credibility factors for one opponent are shown plotted against the enemy's capability for nuclear attack, i.e. an inventory comprising weapons which can be used against all targets, including incendiary devices for large-scale destruction of cities, harvests, etc. The three curves in Fig. 1 illustrate the probable response to three types of attack—namely, against heartland targets, localized attacks against allies but without direct repercussions in home areas and, finally, a peripheral war as an episode of the Cold War.

The slope and shape of the curves are of course purely arbitrary, merely intended to illustrate the likely effect upon country A of the gradual strengthening of country B's nuclear attack potential.

By using advanced war-game techniques it might be possible to assign numerical values to Fig. 1, but this type of study requires a great deal of time and labour and is outside the scope of the present essay. Therefore, Fig. 1 must remain a rough illustration of the basic argument put forward by the

[1] Suggested by General P. Gallois in Chapter 4 of his book *Stratégie de l'Age Nucléaire* (Calmann-Lévy, Paris, 1960).

protagonists of the Western European *independent deterrent* doctrine.

Thus it is not surprising that certain Western European nations attach considerable importance to having retaliatory power without complete dependence upon USA. For instance, it has been suggested that in the event of a local conflict—say over Berlin with a direct threat to West Germany and France —the NATO deterrent credibility may become virtually nil if the "war keys" are hung round the necks of US officers under the direct orders of the Pentagon.

PHASE 4: this will commence when both USA and USSR

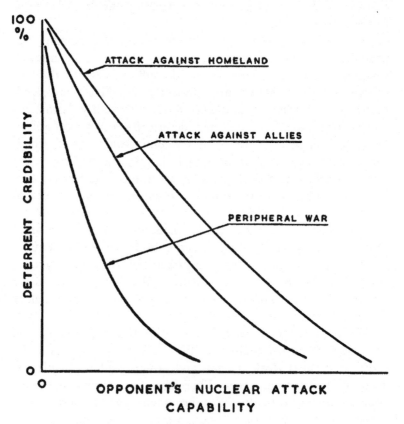

FIG.I. Deterrent credibility.

6

have their full complement of ballistic weapons—either protected or mobile—practically invulnerable to surprise attack. In this respect USA has a certain lead with the *Polaris A-1*, but its range and warload are not adequate to constitute an unquestionable deterrent arm.

It must also be remembered that unforeseeable new developments in the realm of detection and location of submarines could radically alter the situation. On the other hand, it might be said that a further improvement of ballistic missile accuracy might well render the silo or underground installations unacceptably vulnerable; rail systems, such as envisaged for the *Minuteman*, could also be subject to area attacks by nuclear weapons bursting at high altitudes. Nevertheless, in the present state of the art the total mutual elimination of ballistic armaments remains very improbable.

In this connection it may be interesting to study in more detail the survival probabilities of surface ballistic missiles installed in hardened sites, e.g. in underground silos. Leaving aside considerations of cost and complication, it can be assumed that an underground hard site can be designed to withstand overpressures of the order of 100 p.s.i. (lb per sq. inch) or more. It is therefore necessary either to use weapons with very high yields or to improve the accuracy of the missile, both these factors playing a very important role in the *kill capability* of attacking missiles.

It is impossible to compute kill probabilities with accuracy for the simple reason that the information required is of a highly classified nature. Nevertheless, sufficient data have been published to make it possible to evaluate, however roughly, the orders of magnitude involved.[2]

Figure 2 gives a plot of *first-shot kill probabilities* in percentages against unit warhead yields (in kilotons, kt) of the attacking missiles. A third factor is taken into account—namely the *circular probable error* (CEP) expressed in nautical miles, in other words the accuracy of the attacking weapons. Horizontal

[2] *The Effects of Nuclear Weapons*, US Atomic Energy Commission, June 1952; *Missiles and Rockets*, Sept. 19, 1960. See also Appendix II, p. 142.

dotted lines indicate the warhead yield levels mentioned in the technical Press for the *Titan, Atlas, Polaris* and *Minuteman*.[3]

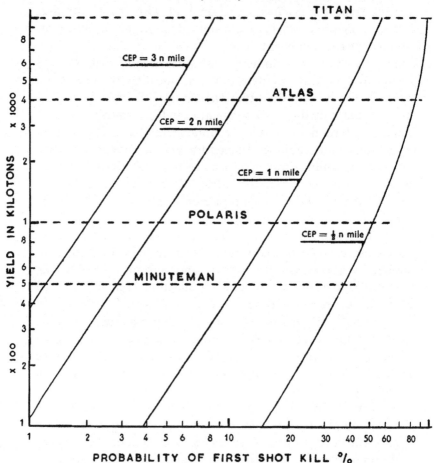

FIG. 2. Effectiveness against hard sites (overpressure 100 p.s.i.).

[3] The warhead yields indicated can be only tentative, since the figures in the technical Press credited to these weapons vary considerably. For instance the *Atlas* is supposed to carry 3 to 6 Mt (megatons); the *Titan* varies from 5 to 7 Mt. *Polaris A-1* and *Minuteman* are believed to have warhead yields of 0.5 Mt, the *Polaris A-2/3* being higher, about 0.6 Mt. In comparison the free-falling bombs of the Boeing *B-52* are reported to be somewhere in the region of 22 to 25 Mt. Alternative sources suggest that taking *Polaris A-1* and *Minuteman* yields as unity, the factors for the *Atlas* and *Titan 2* are 4 and 8 respectively.

A few years ago it was thought that the CEP of an ICBM would be of the order of one-tenth of one per cent. of the range. The latest Press reports indicate that this has been improved and some sources suggest that in three years' time the accuracy of Soviet ICBMs would be nearer to one nautical mile.

Using the probabilities of first-shot kill given in Fig. 2, it is possible to evaluate the fraction of the ballistic missile force expected to survive, in hardened sites, the impact of a salvo of enemy weapons.

Thus, if

S = fraction of attacked ballistic missile force expected to survive,

k = probability of first-shot kill as a fraction of unity,[3a]

r = reliability of attacking missiles as a fraction of unity,

E = number of attacking missiles,

M = number of missiles under attack,

then,

$$S = (1 - k)^{rE/M}.$$

Assuming an overpressure of 100 p.s.i. and CEP = 1 naut. mile, let us consider the case of forty hard sites attacked by 100 ballistic weapons with a unit warhead yield of 1 Mt [4] and r = 0.8. From the formula given above the fraction of the force expected to survive would be approximately 69 per cent.

Repeating the exercise with the same assumptions, but for an attacking warhead unit yield of 25 Mt, the surviving fraction would be reduced to 4½ per cent.

Bearing in mind that an overpressure of some 10 p.s.i. is sufficient to cause major damage to a city, ballistic missiles could be classified under two main headings, namely:

(a) ATTACK OF HARDENED SITES: war-head unit yields of from 5 to 10 Mt.

[3a] See Appendix II, p. 142, for further exposition.

[4] Abbreviations used: Mt = megaton, equivalent to 1 million tons of TNT; kt = kiloton, equivalent to 1 thousand tons of TNT.

(b) ATTACK OF CITIES AND OF SOFT SITES: unit warhead yields of 1 Mt and less.

Figure 2 shows that warhead yields can be traded against CEP, in other words missiles with a high accuracy can be used against hard sites with much lower unit yields. It is thought, however, that in the present state of the art it is probably more expedient to increase the warhead yield and size of the missile than to try to achieve a CEP of half or three-quarters of a nautical mile.

It must also be pointed out that "heavy" warheads have another advantage which makes them more versatile than the smaller calibres; the author has in mind the incendiary technique mentioned further in the present essay and which is supposed to be in considerable favour in USSR.

It is significant that the warheads of *Polaris* and *Minuteman* are likely to be increased, in fact more than doubled.[5]

Thus, it seems that both sides must concentrate their *first waves* of attack on cities and industrial targets. The "mutual blackmail" picture is then complete and both parties are virtually powerless—in fact in a position where no decisive counteraction can be taken to meet a minor political or military *fait accompli* by the opponent—unless suicidal risks are accepted.

Reverting to the possibility of using nuclear weapons for incendiary purposes on a strategic scale,[6] it presupposes the use of high-yield warheads—say in the 10 Mt range—for the mass destruction of means of food production, that is of harvests and cattle. While in USA and Western Europe it is possible to envisage the protection of a part of the population from high-altitude flash effects, coupled with large-scale storage of foodstuffs, the latter countermeasure is largely outside the present-day capabilities of USSR and China. In a major nuclear exchange —populations on both sides having a measure of protection against high bursts—Communist countries would be more vulnerable to the threat of mass starvation. It was estimated

---

[5] *Missiles and Rockets*, March 6, 1961.

[6] Suggested by C. Rougeron in various articles: e.g. in *L'Air*, January 1955 and January 1957.

that USA could store, without difficulty, food reserves for about two years; this is quite beyond the capacity of its potential opponents.

Eventually, fire-raising on a strategic scale could be combined with aerospace weapons. Since the impact accuracy of early forms of de-orbited devices may not be very great, their employment for mass incendiary effects would greatly increase the deterrent potential. In fact, it might provide a reasonably dissuasive form of posthumous retaliation.

*

It is thus conceivable that the next few years will be a trying period for "minor Powers", allies and satellites of USA and USSR. The two leaders could well pursue a policy of *fait accompli*; however serious aggressions may be—so long as they are outside the territories of the two principals—any drastic reaction would mean virtual suicide. Thus, as a result of the strategic stalemate, Cold War political action might become more violent, both sides realizing that if the opposing armaments cannot be effectively neutralized cities and industrial targets would be under threat of immediate destruction.

Finally, an important point is that these armaments will, in fact, be controlled by a few people. To be effective, modern weapons must be used very quickly, possibly without warning; in other words there may not be sufficient time to obtain what is known as *popular approval*. Historically it puts the clock back to a sort of medieval pattern of events where the fate of large communities depended upon the wisdom or stupidity of a feudal *élite*.

*

The failures of both the Paris Summit Conference of 1960 and of the much more discreet Kennedy-Khrushchev 1961 meeting in Vienna point to the inadequacy of "high level" talks, particularly in an atmosphere of *low deterrent credibility*. In addition, there are many hidden motives operating behind the

Iron Curtain that can nullify the effectiveness of such talks, even if they are made to look successful and do not result in spectacular, widely-publicized breakdowns. Russo-Chinese differences, though openly mentioned in the Western Press, can also be classified under the broad heading of "occult influences".

Thus there may be a great deal to be said in favour of old "secret diplomacy" methods which allow both sides to bargain and seek a solution without theatrical performances designed to humiliate the opponents.

The position with regard to disarmament and nuclear test agreements may eventually improve. The resumption of nuclear tests by the Soviets in autumn 1961 culminating in the 50-megaton burst on October 30, does not necessarily mean that talks on the limitation of atomic armaments will not be resumed after the completion of the series. Naturally the Western Allies will be much less receptive and, in the meantime, USA would be fully justified, on strategic grounds, in going through with its own test programme.

While the "Big U" may still require additional data on the effects of nuclear weapons, particularly those of the high-neutron yield kind, unless some form of nuclear agreement is arrived at there remains the twofold risk of increasing pollution of the atmosphere beyond an acceptable limit and of secondary Powers acquiring restricted atomic armaments sufficient to enable them to create additional political crises in particularly sensitive areas.

Thus, is it not in the interests of the three Powers at present possessing atomic weapons to have new applicants to the "Nuclear Club". This became fairly obvious when the French exploded their first A-bomb early in 1960. It must be remembered, however, that France is regarded as a "responsible" nation and nobody in his right mind would expect General de Gaulle to start a preventive nuclear war.

The position would be different if some minor and irresponsible nation were to achieve independent manufacture of atomic weapons. It would constitute a threat to the major Powers, since a local incident between two minor states, involving the use of nuclear armaments, could well explode into a global conflict. For instance, reports that the French Government intend to help Israel to develop its own nuclear weapons are somewhat alarming. The USSR would be automatically compelled either to supply atomic arms to the United Arab Republic or else guarantee Syria's and Egypt's safety against possible Israeli action. Under the new régime of *fait accompli* the Soviets could go much further and create an incident in the Middle East, without clearly defined responsibilities. It is unlikely that the US Government could intervene effectively at the risk of bringing chaos and destruction to its own "Heartland".

*

One of the major unknowns is the attitude of Communist China. According to recent reports the Chinese Government is pressing on with the development of nuclear weapons, at first with Soviet help. It was also suggested that Mao Tse Tung's followers optimistically consider that their country can withstand a nuclear attack, or at least emerge from a World War in a better condition than the other great Powers. This is a highly debatable assumption: the Chinese leaders do not seem to appreciate their country's vulnerability to radiation and bacteriological forms of modern warfare. It is thought, however, that a better understanding of the situation will prevail, possibly with the aid of the USSR Government, who, after all, will derive no discernible benefit from being unwittingly dragged into a nuclear war by the political and strategic ineptitude of an ally. In fact, on June 26, 1960 at the Communist Congress in Bucharest, Mr. Khrushchev told the Chinese that they knew nothing about modern war.[7]

The *81 Communist Parties' Agreement* concluded in Moscow in November 1960 was supposed to ensure ideological peace between Moscow and Peking. It spoke in favour of "peaceful co-existence", but in accordance with Chinese wishes it also committed USSR to fight against the "export of counter-

[7] *The Observer*, London, February 12, 1961.

revolution by Western Imperialism". In return, Mao Tse Tung promised not to obstruct Khrushchev's diplomatic efforts and stop charging him with weakness and appeasing USA.

By mid-1961 an argument flared up: Moscow accused Peking of having violated almost every point of the agreement. The Chinese were accused of surreptitious propaganda against the principles of the Moscow Declaration, in the first instance against "peaceful co-existence". Peking was further charged with conducting intrigues against Moscow in Europe, Asia and Africa.

Khrushchev also blamed Mao Tse Tung for "being obsessed with Formosa" and "bent on liberating Formosa" at the risk of a World War.[8]

These reports, even if they are only partly accurate, indicate a serious rift between the Russians and the Chinese. It also suggests that the Kremlin fully realizes the risks involved in a major nuclear war and, presumably, the disadvantages of a common land frontier with the former Celestial Empire.

The latest differences of opinion between USSR and Red China confirm the impression of a major rift between these two Powers. It may be that the explosion of the Soviet "50-Mt plus" device was, in fact, intended as a hidden warning to allies —as well as to enemies and neutrals.

Nevertheless, the only real *Third Force* is Red China. The future attitude and policies of the Mao Tse Tung régime are impossible to forecast, but one of its aims seems to be the prevention of any form of "peaceful co-existence" between East and West. This puts USSR in a difficult position, since, in the final analysis, it is not in the interests of Russia as a nation to encourage the free expansion of the successors of the former Celestial Empire. The climatic conditions in Siberia are not ideal for mass immigration from China, particularly from its southern provinces, but the Old Silk Road is an obvious overflow channel for an overpopulated and increasingly aggressive nation. While there are other routes of expansion— e.g. south towards India and into areas formerly known as

[8] *The Sunday Times*, London, July 2, 1961.

Indo-China—it is quite conceivable that Sino-Russian interests will eventually clash in the Middle East. This explains the acute competition between USSR and Communist China in Arab countries along the southern Mediterranean coast. Here Russians are under a disadvantage because of the traditional enmity of the Moslems. The latter had no political and religious feuds with the Chinese, who undoubtedly will do their utmost to exploit this advantage.

While there is a distinct possibility of an eventual Sino-Russian clash, it is highly unlikely that the Soviets would or could enlist Western help. The alternative may be that the Russians will be compelled to resolve the conflict with the West by force in order to be free to deal with the Chinese threat at some later date. This is, of course, an extremely risky plan; only a fully-successful preventive nuclear attack against USA could enable the USSR to turn against a China not directly affected by an atomic intercontinental war.

After a broad examination of the general political situation, it might be of interest to mention the part played in world affairs by UK-Commonwealth, other West European NATO partners and what is known as "uncommitted" nations. Leaving aside cultural and economic qualifications, attention will be focused upon their respective military potentials.

The world trend towards the abolition of "colonialism" has resulted in a political reconstruction of major Powers with possessions and zones of influence spread over several continents. While the British Commonwealth and the French Communauté represent a very considerable cultural and economic force, it is evident that their military powers cannot be compared with those of geographically self-contained first-rank nations. This is inescapable, since modern technology and industry call for an increasing degree of concentration of means of production and highly centralized control. Moreover, the absence of exposed lines of communication improves the strategic posture of self-contained political units. Previously, naval forces and merchant shipping could compensate for geographical dispersal, but the advent of nuclear power—both as motive power and as an explosive—made sea routes very vulnerable.

In an emergency the British Commonwealth would have to rely on air transport for the movement of army vanguards and essential logistic supplies. Among others, this poses the difficult problem of intermediate staging points, namely the possibility of their "neutralization" due to adverse political circumstances. For example, elimination of Gan in the Indian Ocean would disrupt lines of communication bypassing the Middle East.

Therefore, in a major conflict both the British Commonwealth and the Communauté Française must have the co-operation of US Armed Forces. A very important form of strategic support would be air control over certain areas and logistic transport by specialized units of USAF.

On the other hand, Britain and France may be called upon to play an important part in the prevention or early suppression of peripheral conflicts. Consequently one of the essential features of British and French strategic plans must be the formation of powerful air-mobile army units capable of intervening in outlying areas in the shortest possible time. This important contribution would relieve demands imposed upon the US strategic forces, whose main role should be the neutralization of intervention threats on the part of USSR.

The introduction of more sophisticated weapon systems— e.g. orbitals—will tend to emphasize the difference between the strategic tasks facing the UK and France on the one hand and the USA on the other. This does not mean that the British Commonwealth and Western European NATO Powers need not take any interest in aerospace armaments, but it does mean that their efforts in this particular field will be limited by industrial and financial considerations.

There appears to be a minority opinion in Western Europe advocating the adoption of a policy of virtual neutrality. The word *neutralism* is seldom heard, but somewhat similar tendencies appeared under the disguise of an alleged *Third Force*. From the economic point of view it is quite reasonable to regard Western Europe, including Britain, as a single unit with a very considerable industrial potential, but strategically speaking the concept is fundamentally unsound.

Effective defence against nuclear and biological weapons presupposes the existence of an adequate hinterland, if only to make it possible to disperse a part of the population under the threat of a full-scale atomic onslaught. From the Soviet angle a neutral European "Third Force" cannot constitute a military threat; in fact, it would only strengthen the Communist posture. Assuming Western Europe remained neutral in a war between USA and USSR, it would be naïve to imagine that in the event of victory the latter could tolerate the continued existence of a conglomeration of potentially hostile states. The concept of an *uncommitted* Western Europe is a fallacy and can only delude public opinion into a feeling of false security.

Finally, a few words about "uncommitted" nations, including new political formations in Asia and Africa. In terms of manpower resources some of these post-World War II nations may look impressive, but their military potential on a global scale is, to put it politely, highly problematical.

It is, of course, possible that risings or interstate wars, say in Africa, would require considerable forces to bring them under control. Nevertheless, the fact remains that it is more than unlikely that India, Indonesia, Ghana, or Madagascar could eventually play a significant part in a world-wide nuclear war. These nations could only come into their own if the Western Hemisphere were neutralized by casualties, damage and radioactive fall-out virtually eliminating USA, Western Europe and USSR from the political scene.

In addition, a number of uncommitted non-European nations, particularly those of recent formation, are economically weak and their political structure often insecure. Therefore, in the overall pattern of Grand Strategy, these areas should be considered mainly as possible theatres of peripheral wars and incidents; in an all-out atomic clash between USA and USSR, their allies and satellites, the military posture of the majority of uncommitted nations would be of little consequence.

CHAPTER II

Transition from Air to Aerospace

The evolution of strategic air and aerospace weapons is a very complex process depending upon the progress of science and technology in areas controlled by military requirements which are often in a fluid state.

The case history of the strategic arm of the USAF will be reviewed to illustrate this process of evolution—from manned bombers to strategic missiles and, eventually, into orbital systems. The Strategic Air Command (SAC) of USAF offers the best-known example of the gradual transformation of an aggregate of major air formations which had achieved a commanding position in World Power Politics.

In the preparation of the present chapter the writer made extensive use of the excellent review of SAC activities in the US periodical *Aviation Week*.[1] This article provides a sound basis for the study of the evolutionary process which will eventually transform the strategic concepts inherited from World War II.

For the first fifteen years of its existence SAC relied on a single type of weapon—long-range aircraft carrying nuclear bombs. During this period a unique line of development was pursued, expressed in terms of improved performance and payload.

Originally a long-range Bomber Command, SAC is now beginning its transmutation into a *Strategic Aerospace Force*. Its primary duty is to deter any potential aggressor from embark-

[1] "SAC in Transition", *Aviation Week*, pp. 101–44, June 20, 1960.

PLATE 1. *Atlas* booster: with *Agena* second stage and *Midas* satellite (left);
with *Mercury* capsule (right).

[facing p. 18]

PLATE 2. Martin *Titan* ICBM.

[facing p. 19]

ing on ventures that could result in a world-wide conflagration. Consequently, there is great urgency in developing and integrating new weapon systems into an *aerospace force-in-being*. Considerable skill will be required in the deployment and use of this force, short of armed conflict.

If deterrence fails, SAC's main task is to win an unavoidable war.

In 1960 SAC controlled over 90 per cent. of the TNT-equivalent of the nuclear striking power of the Western Block. To achieve this SAC absorbed about 20 per cent. of the total annual US defence budget; it comprised 10 per cent. of the total number of aircraft and 7 per cent. of the Armed Forces' personnel. Over 90 per cent. of SAC's nuclear delivery potential was represented by some two thousand *B-47*[2] medium and *B-52*[3] heavy jet bombers.

In 1960 the bulk of SAC formations consisted of *B-47*s, but these obsolescent medium jet bombers and the obsolete piston-engine *KC-97* tankers were being phased out. The first B-47 was delivered in 1951; SAC built up a force of about 1,800 before the rundown to the 1960 level of some 1,400 aircraft began.

While the *B-47* declines, the *B-52* force is still growing. The bulk of the 744 *B-52*s of the 1960 programme have been delivered, but new models are still coming into the inventory; with the aid of weapons such as *Hound Dog* and *Skybolt*, the life of this heavy bomber is expected to extend beyond the 1960s.

The first squadrons of supersonic *B-58*[4] bombers are now in transition training. This medium type is intended to replace the *B-47*, but present plans do not envisage its deployment overseas.

Organizationally a strategic wing includes fifteen *B-52* bombers and ten *KC-135* tankers. Dispersal of strategic wings helps to meet the requirement that no more than one *B-52*

[2] Boeing *B-47*: typical range over 3,000 miles with an-18 Mt warload.
[3] Boeing *B-52*: typical range 10,000 miles with a 20-Mt warload; *H series* may be up to 70 Mt (*Aviation Report*, May 26, 1961).
[4] Convair *B-58*: typical range over 3,000 miles with a 15-Mt warload.

squadron of fifteen aircraft is stationed at any particular base. As the *B-47* is phased out, the remaining medium bombers may be combined into wings stronger than the present forty-five aircraft.

As a result of the introduction of the *B-52*, SAC was able to begin the withdrawal from its overseas bases, concentrating the majority of long-range bombers in continental USA. Some *B-47* overseas stations are being maintained, but they will also serve as recovery points for crippled SAC aircraft. The main problem is to ensure SAC's survival in the event of a surprise attack. The heavy bomber fleet is based behind three radar warning nets—the DEW Line covering the polar cap, the mid-Canada Line and the Pine Tree Lines across the northern tier of USA. The Atlantic and Pacific flanks are protected by *Texas Towers* and airborne radar units.

This warning net should give SAC at least two to three hours warning of an attack by manned aircraft; thus a normal alert status is sufficient at advanced bases in Europe, Alaska, Guam and Africa. The fact that the NATO system could give a fifteen-minute warning is also taken into account.

With SAC's system of positive control it is possible to launch the bomber fleets without waiting for incontrovertible evidence of an enemy attack, and retain the possibility of automatic return if the *go-code* is not received by the airborne forces within a certain period of time. The decision to transmit the *go-code*—from the President through the Joint Chiefs of Staff to SAC H.Q.—can be delayed before the automatic recall point is reached.

The advent of Soviet ICBMs had a profound effect on the situation. As matters stand at present SAC would get little or no warning of a ballistic missile attack. Even with the completion of the Ballistic Missile Early Warning System (BMEWs), there would be no certainty of a fifteen-minute warning to permit adaptation of SAC's bomber reaction to this margin.[5]

[5] In Financial Year 1962 budget additional funds are provided for an expansion of the present *15-minute Ground Alert Force* from one-third to one-half of the total number of bombers.

Thus, SAC face the task of developing survival tactics effective without any warning. To meet the requirement, the *airborne alert* concept was developed and tests made of keeping up to 25 per cent. of the heavy bomber forces in the air at all times, out of reach of surprise attack by ICBMs. The exact percentage of the alert force has not been disclosed, but it may be of the order of one-third. All this means more spare engines, electronic gear and other spares, additional crews for both tankers and bombers and, finally, a heavy expenditure of fuel.

In terms of money the airborne alert is an expensive countermeasure. In the 1960 Financial Year the Defense Department has allocated $85 million for spares and $15 million for alert training; sums of $60 million and $25 million respectively were assigned for these purposes in the 1961 financial year. The annual cost of actually flying an alert with one-eighth of the *B-52* force would amount to $225 million, in addition to current *B-52* and *KC-135* operating expenses.

For the type of airborne alert SAC wish to implement $492 million would have to be added to the original Financial Year 1961 budget request. This would cover more spares, extra crews and the necessary training expenses. Once the required capability were attained for a quarter of the *B-52* force, it would cost some $800 million per annum in addition to funds now allocated to *B-52* bombers and *KC-135* tankers.

This was the position towards the end of 1960. Since then there have been changes in US strategic planning: the Joint Chiefs of Staff decided to recommend a one-year postponement in the phasing out of the Boeing *B-47* medium bomber wings. The explanation of this move, suggested in the American technical Press, was the unsatisfactory Circular Error Probability of operational *Atlas* missiles in their present form and the poor record of *Polaris* launches from submerged submarines. At the time the decision was made the *Polaris* record was ten successes in eighteen shots. Later modifications were made to the missiles and the success rate rose to twelve successes in twenty launches.

Actually the Boeing *B-47* phase-down from twenty to thirteen wings by the end of June 1961 will not be halted, but further reductions will be suspended, provided the recommendations of the Joint Chiefs of Staff are accepted.

*

The above brief review of manned aircraft operations must be supplemented by a summary of the growth and organization of Strategic Missile Forces.

The present deployment of *Atlas* and *Titan* ICBMs offers little in the way of counterattack potential—even with an authentic fifteen-minute warning—since it is highly improbable that an order to launch the missiles would be given before actual impacts were recorded on US soil. Thus, the liquid-fuelled ICBMs would have to ride out the first enemy missile salvo; the sites must be hardened and dispersed so that the surviving *Atlases* and *Titans* can follow and overtake the airborne alert force on its way to enemy targets.

General Power stated that this relatively small target system could be crippled by a strike of approximately 300 missiles (150 IRBMs and 150 ICBMs), allowing three shots to each target to achieve a 90 per cent. probability of destroying the installation. At that time there was no incontrovertible evidence that USSR actually had 150 ICBMs on pads and General Power used this only as a hypothetical example of the danger of the present situation. Evidently, as explained in Chapter I, hardened and dispersed US ballistic missile sites would greatly increase the opponent's surprise attack requirements.

The switch to all-inertial guidance allows of a nine-site *Atlas* squadron, each individual missile located at such an interval as to make vital damage to more than one site per enemy missile hit unlikely. This *Atlas* deployment is an evolutionary step toward the twelve-missile squadron, with each missile encased in a concrete silo built to withstand anything but a direct hit by a multi-megaton warhead. Coming after the *Atlas*, the *Titan* will begin directly in hardened silos and dispersed installations that also harden the guidance system antenna. Later *Titan* squadrons will switch to all-inertial guidance and utilize storable non-cryogenic fuels which will improve the reaction time and make possible underground firing from the silo.

Thus SAC's second priority, next to the airborne alert, is to expand the size, hardening and dispersal of its ICBM force in 1962–63, when additional *Atlas* production could be translated into a greater number of hard-site units.

By the mid-1960s SAC will be approaching an important transition phase. Its initial striking power will be almost equally distributed between the bomber fleet with air-launched missiles and the ICBMs in the *Atlas* and *Titan* complexes. With this mixed force-in-being, the US Command should be able to bring in an additional deterrent factor—the solid-fuelled, hard-sited *Minuteman*. This new ICBM, with its relatively low cost, long storability and very short reaction time, will complicate the opponent's target problem. Further difficulties will be created by the mobility of certain *Minuteman* units, for instance by the use of missile trains moving at random over the western US network of railways.

The planned deployment of US ballistic missiles is shown in Table 1 (pp. 24–5).[6] Some of the weapons listed are illustrated in Plates 1, 2, 3 and 4 (facing pp. 18, 19, 34 and 35).

The USAF Ballistic Missile Division is developing operational techniques for the initial *Minuteman* installations. This missile can be launched by in-silo firings from hardened, widely dispersed, thirty- or fifty-weapon squadron sites, or from special railway trains.

The mobile *Minuteman* system calls for five weapons to be carried by train and deployed over 900 to 1,500 miles of railway track, a mobile squadron consisting of six to ten trains. Pre-computed launch points will be designated along the rail lines and the trains shifted in a random pattern to preclude any possibility of the missiles being targeted for initial destruction.

The *Minuteman* period will correspond to a major shift from

[6] Based on information published in *Aviation Week*, June 20, 1960; *Missiles and Rockets*, June 6, 1960; *Aviation Week*, November 21, 1960; *Missiles and Rockets*, July 17, 1961.

TABLE I   Planned deployment of US ballistic missiles (mid-1961)

Convair Atlas

Base (AFB)	Location	No. of sqdns.	Site configuration	Total missiles
Vandenberg	Santa Maria, Calif.	1	Soft	10
Warren	Cheyenne, Wyo.	1	Soft 3 × 2	6
ditto	ditto	1	Soft 3 × 3	9
ditto	ditto	1	Semi-hard 3 × 3	9
Offutt	Omaha, Neb.	1	Soft 3 × 3	9
Fairchild	Spokane, Wash.	1	Semi-hard 1 × 9	9
Forbes	Topeka, Kan.	1	Semi-hard 1 × 12	12
Schilling	Salina, Kan.	1	Hard 1 × 12	12
Lincoln	Lincoln, Neb.	1	Hard 1 × 9	9
Walker	Roswell, N.M.	1	Hard 1 × 12	12
Dyess	Abilene, Tex.	1	Hard 1 × 12	12
Altus	Altus, Okla.	1	Hard 1 × 12	12
Plattsburgh	Plattsburgh, N.Y.	1	Hard 1 × 12	12
			Total	133†

Martin Titan I

Base (AFB)	Location	No. of sqdns.	Site configuration	Total missiles
Lowry	Denver, Colo.	2	Hard 3 × 3	18
Beale	Marysville, Calif.	1	Hard 3 × 3	9
Mountain Home	Mountain Home, Idaho	1	Hard 3 × 3	9
Larson	Moses Lake, Wash.	1	Hard 3 × 3	9
Ellsworth	Rapid City, S.D.	1	Hard 3 × 3	9

24

Martin Titan 2

Davis-Monthan .	.	Tucson, Ariz.	2	Hard 1 × 9	18
McConnell .	.	Wichita, Kan.	2	Hard 1 × 9	18
Little Rock .	.	Little Rock, Ark.	2	Hard 1 × 9	18
		Total			108

Boeing Minuteman

Malmstrom .	.	Great Falls, Mont.	3	Hard	150
Ellsworth .	.	S.D.	3	Hard, dispersed	150
Hill .	.	Utah	Railhead of mobile squadrons		
Minot .	.	N.D.	3	Hard, dispersed	150
Whiteman .	.	Mo.	3	Hard, dispersed	150
		Total			600

Lockheed Polaris

Total number of submarines: 29*		
Missiles per submarine	.	16
	Total	464

* Total planned by USN: 45 submarines.

† Press reports suggest that by the end of October 1961 USAF would have 48 operational *Atlases* (*Missiles and Rockets*, September 26, 1961).

25

the bomb bays of manned vehicles to the warheads of fixed and mobile ICBMs. Considerable reduction in the cost of the solid-fuelled *Minuteman* as compared with the larger, more complex, liquid-fuelled, first generation ICBMs will enable the USAF to deploy this weapon in sufficient quantities to present a virtually insoluble target problem to any potential enemy.

The following unit missile costs will help to illustrate this point:[7]

Atlas, in hardened 1 × 12 dispersed squadron configuration — $13.7 million.

Minuteman, per silo — $3.4 million.

Aircraft maintenance largely works on the theory that 10 to 25 per cent. of the force may be grounded at any one time for scheduled and unscheduled maintenance. With missiles, due to the limited number of launching sites available and the requirement for a fifteen-minute readiness, an *in-commission rate* near 100 per cent. is required.

Early in the ICBM programme an effort was made by Convair and USAF to establish the number of items in the weapon system needing periodic inspection. The total arrived at was 10,474; it soon became evident that such a workload, coupled with the requirement for frequent calibration of various components, would make it impossible to achieve an acceptable launch readiness. Finally, USAF and Convair succeeded in cutting down the number of inspection items to 3,010.

Calibration of the many sensing devices of the missile system and of its ground support equipment imposes a very heavy workload on the maintenance staff. SAC personnel frankly admitted that the magnitude of the calibration requirements had not been recognized in the early stages of establishing the maintenance routine. Eventually, as a result of careful scrutiny, these requirements were reduced by 40 per cent.

Maintenance procedures will change in the case of the inertially-guided *Atlas E* dispersed 1 × 9 sites, mainly due to simplified propellant loading procedures and elimination of the guidance centre.

[7] *Missiles and Rockets*, December 12, 1960.

Finally, while on the subject of maintenance, checking and control, it must be appreciated that the increasing complexity of ICBM launch installations, evolving into virtually automated systems, will increase the danger of war by accident. An up-to-date missile launching pad or silo comprises a vast number of electronic decision-making systems which can be understood and looked after only by those who actually designed each particular segment of the installation. Ways have been detected and corrected in which chains of unwanted electronic events could have launched missiles; it is therefore obvious that when ICBMs are deployed in transitional stages and electronics are continually being modified, there cannot be an absolute certainty that all undesirable pulses have been forestalled.[7a] Therefore the bizarre, but logical, conclusion is that the arrival of one or several missiles does not necessarily mean war. The difficulty would be to convince a potential enemy that this is a sort of hazard he will have to put up with and refrain from taking drastic retaliatory action if one or several of his cities were blasted to smithereens as a result of an electronic error.

*

Beyond the "Missile Gap" period, SAC will need new bombers to maintain a modern manned attack force, considered to be the most flexible element of the future *missile-bomber mix*.[8] As the missile force grows and the bomber force declines in numbers the total SAC mix should reach a fifty-fifty balance by 1965. At that point the role of manned aircraft will be reassessed for the period during which large numbers of *Minuteman* and *Polaris*

[7a] *Aviation Report*, No. 1066, October 27, 1961.

[8] The 1960 *missile-bomber mix* was estimated at:

OPERATIONAL MISSILES:		OPERATIONAL BOMBERS:	
Atlas (SAC)	12	*B-47* (SAC)	over 1,000
Polaris (USN)	16	*B-52* (SAC)	550
Snark (SAC)	20	*B-58* (SAC)	12
Matador and *Mace* (TAC)	250	Carrier bombers (USN)	400
		Fighter bombers (USAF)	2,000

(*Missiles and Rockets*, November 14, 1960).

weapons are dispersed to form the main deterrent structure. New supersonic bombers such as the North American *B-70 Valkyrie*[9] and space weapon systems will begin to appear on the scene. For instance, according to Press reports, given adequate financial support the first SAC *B-70* wing could be equipped by autumn 1966.[10]

*

There are few reliable indications in the Press as to the deployment of Soviet ballistic weapons. In autumn 1960 *Die Bundeswehr*, a monthly West German publication, gave a report on the supposed location of launching sites.

According to this journal, USSR had ten permanent sites from which ICBMs with ranges of 5,000 miles could be launched against USA. Thirty more permanent launching bases, armed with IRBMs (intermediate-range ballistic missiles) of 1,500 miles range, are said to cover targets in Great Britain, Western Europe, North Africa, the Middle East, Alaska, Okinawa, Formosa and Red China. It is also stated that Western Intelligence Services have discovered a missile site "between two inaccessible mountain plateaux in Kamchatka equipped with rockets of 3,000 miles range which appear to be directed only against Communist China". Reasons for this deduction were not given.

A mobile launching base operating out of the Kola Peninsula was observed moving along the railway lines in that area. The only large missile site outside the Soviet Union was described as being located at Seroc, in Poland; it is supposedly armed with IRBMs.

Estimates from other sources [11] suggested that by the end of the first half of 1961 the Soviets had thirty-five to fifty long-range missiles ready for firing. Locations of thirty-seven

[9] There is also a project for using the *B-70* as Recoverable Booster Space System (RBSS), possibly in conjunction with *DynaSoar*, *Samos* and *Midas* (*Missiles and Rockets*, August 29, 1960).

[10] *Aviation Week*, August 8, 1960.

[11] *US News and World Report*, May 29, 1961.

launching pads appear to have been pinpointed: nine ICBM sites, the rest IRBM installations.

It was also suggested that in winter 1961–62 USSR would have produced up to 200 strategic missiles. In Fig. 3 the total deployment of Soviet ICBMs approximates to 150; it is thought

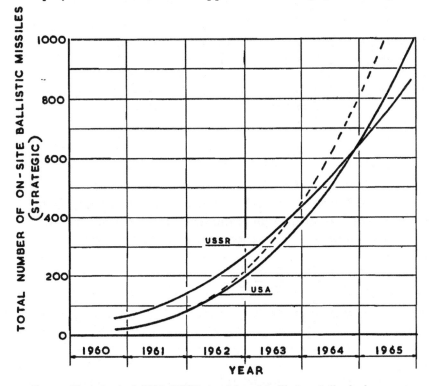

FIG. 3. Hypothetical USA-USSR land-based ballistic missile deployment.

that in the prevailing state of uncertainty these two figures are in reasonably good agreement.

From the point of view of comparative strengths of USA and USSR long-range ballistic forces (ICBMs and FBMs), estimates of the so-called *Missile Gap* have appeared in the Press, allegedly based on comments and information released by the American Department of Defense.[12] The curves drawn in full lines in

[12] For instance, *Newsweek*, October 24, 1960.

Fig. 3 are to some extent hypothetical, "smoothed out" to illustrate the average rate of build-up of US and USSR strategic missile armaments. The dotted line corresponds to a more recent estimate based on the Financial Year 1962 US budget trends, namely 1,300 missiles by 1965. This tallies with the total of Table 1.

By 1966 the *Atlas* and *Titan 1* should have been withdrawn, the latter superseded by the storable liquid-propellant *Titan 2* with a much shorter reaction time:[13]

Titan 2 . . .	276
Minuteman . . .	1,000
Polaris . . .	474
Total . . .	1,750

In the course of the last revision of US budgets the Defense Secretary, Robert S. McNamara, ordered the costing of the entire nuclear weapon programmes up to Financial Year 1967. The total number of strategic missiles envisaged was:

Minuteman ICBM (fixed) . . .	2,500
Minuteman ICBM (mobile) . . .	415
Titan ICBM	275
Polaris FBM	720
Total . .	3,910

This more than doubles the total number of missiles in a period prolonged by one year. The cost of such an overall programme is mentioned in Chapter IV.[14]

*

The first phase of the development of space systems will include surveillance devices for early warning, photo and electronic

[13] *Aviation Week*, April 3, 1961.
[14] *Aviation Week*, July 24, 1961.

reconnaissance orbitals with swift and continuous data transmission characteristics.

The recent launches of *Midas* and *Tiros* satellites confirm the trend towards the extension of strategic armaments and of their ancillary systems into orbital space.

The manned aircraft section of this phase will be composed of several new weapon systems with improved flexibility and survival potential; this will include the *B-70* Mach-3 bomber for armed reconnaissance and strikes with air-launched ballistic missiles. Finally, the Boeing *DynaSoar* orbital bomber may be the first US manned true aerospace weapon system.

". . . We may think in terms of space," said General Power, C.-in-C., SAC, USAF, "although space is merely a medium and not a weapon. But as air supremacy meant control of the battleground beneath in World War II, control of space may well mean control of the globe in a future war. Hence, the conquest of space is more than a race for scientific 'firsts' and national prestige.

"Whether we like it or not, it is still primarily a question of survival.

"No one can foretell what problems will arise in extending our defences hundreds of thousands of miles above the ground which we are dedicated to protect. But it is not beyond the realm of possibility that this may require manned spacecraft which would orbit the earth in a continuous space alert.

"Their purpose would be threefold—to provide instant warning of any act of aggression, to intercept hostile missiles and spacecraft, and above all to deter aggressions as heretofore. . . ."[15]

An important qualification must be introduced from the start. While it is not proposed to look farther than the orbital space surrounding the Earth, it is possible that even this comparatively narrow manoeuvring space can be reduced by the presence of radiation belts or zones. Satellite observations have confirmed the existence of the *Van Allen belts*; more recent

[15] *Aviation Week*, June 20, 1960.

31

indications have been obtained about other forms of radiation, including the effects of solar flares.

This raises a very important question, namely, whether human beings can be exposed to the danger of accumulated doses or lethal bursts of radiation from sources such as disturbances on the surface of the sun. High intensities may prevent space travel, at least until such time as new forms of shielding are devised which are not subject to unacceptable weight penalties. From this particular point of view it is doubtful if the USSR manned-satellite flights have provided much in the way of basic information.

To achieve the systems envisaged in Chapter V it is not really necessary to consider orbits higher than 500 miles, i.e. under the canopy of the first Van Allen belt. Moreover, the simpler forms of aerospace weapons need not be manned, so that the question of radiation hazards will not arise to its full extent.

*

The pattern of evolution of SAC is plainly discernible, and a somewhat similar tendency, though on a much more modest scale, was observed within NATO [16] and in the independent French plans to organize a striking force including a proportion of ballistic weapons. In the latter case it remains to be seen whether the country's economy can stand the strain of such expenditure, bearing in mind General de Gaulle's declared intention to rely on French-designed and -produced nuclear warheads. Moreover, this strike force must be built up quickly

[16] Earlier NATO plans reportedly envisaged the use of ballistic missiles on a strategic scale. While Britain and France maintain their independent strike forces, SHAPE would establish three arcs of missile bases manned by crews from all NATO countries. The first line would consist of 500-mile range *Pershings* arrayed across W. Germany; farther back, *Polaris* missiles would be strung out from the Low Countries to Turkey. Finally, an arc of *Minuteman* ICBMs would make up the third line (*Newsweek*, October 3, 1960).

The original US proposal to provide NATO with five *Polaris* submarines, on condition that member nations purchase a further 100 missiles to be deployed at sea by 1964, appears to have been abandoned (*Daily Telegraph*, London, April 3, 1961).

to be politically effective; this means drastic reductions in lead times of the weapon systems envisaged; which is a very costly enterprise.

The terminal evolution of manned bombers will also depend upon geographical factors—for instance, whether their bases are within striking distance of enemy ICBMs or IRBMs. It is self-evident that the time of flight of ballistic weapons is an essential factor in the determination of the required readiness of aircraft, to afford reasonable chances of survival in the event of a surprise attack by long-range missiles.

Even in the case of ICBMs, with flight times of the order of thirty minutes, the USAF consider it necessary to maintain some form of partial airborne alert. Published information is not sufficient to indicate whether the various systems of anti-missile warnings, with the exception of orbitals, can give anything like the time required for the totality of SAC units to become airborne before the impact of enemy ballistic weapons.

The position becomes much more difficult in the case of IRBMs, i.e. in theatres of war where the striking ranges are in the region of 1,000 miles or less. The time of flight of an IRBM is evidently much shorter than that of an ICBM, and this has a very pronounced adverse effect on the survival probabilities of ground-sited reprisal bombers.

The British Government appear to be quite satisfied with the defence plans now in force. No doubt there are good reasons for this display of confidence, as otherwise the "face lifting" of RAF strategic bombers to accept the Douglas *Skybolt* would not be justified.

There is, however, one point which raises some doubts in the mind of an independent observer.[17] There are indications that Soviet weapon specialists think in terms of high-altitude nuclear bursts, the main object being to enhance the incendiary

---

[17] A very interesting editorial, under the heading "It is time to disband the Royal Air Force", in *Aeronautics* (London), February 1961, raises a number of points in connection with the declared policies of H.M. Government.

effect of a multi-megaton deflagration over a given area. High-altitude weapons might also be used against air bases. Consequently, reprisal aircraft must not only be airborne by the time the enemy missiles reach the bomber stations,[18] but have to be sufficiently far away to avoid thermal damage or expose their crews to an intense radiation flux. The results of the *Project Argus* experiment suggest that at great altitudes, where the air screening is very much reduced, semi-lethal doses of radiation can be absorbed by crews within distances of the order of 100 miles from the point of explosion of a megaton-class weapon.

Last but not least, nuclear high-altitude explosions are likely to disrupt the radio-location and communications systems —a most undesirable side-effect in the event of an emergency.

For obvious geographical reasons, it might be safer to assume that in Europe only airborne bombers will survive a sudden and massive onslaught of medium-range ballistic weapons. At present, the known countermeasures are airborne alert and dispersal, which means flight refuelling and operations from distant bases. This is an expensive form of deployment, but a further improvement of ballistic missile performance and new forms of attack will make it mandatory—otherwise money spent on "face lifting" of existing bombers and on the introduction of air-launched ballistic missiles (ALBMs) might well prove to be a very poor investment.

Thus, in the particular instance of Western Europe, it seems more logical and more in keeping with modern trends to build the reprisal potential upon some form of less-vulnerable weapons such as the Lockheed *Polaris* or Boeing *Minuteman*. It is also evident that in the former case non-American members of NATO cannot afford a sufficient number of nuclear submarines,[19] but there are other ways of using FBMs in a much

[18] In 1960, 30 per cent. of SAC (about 700 *B-47*s and *B-52*s) had achieved a ground readiness of fifteen minutes. The reaction time of the *Atlas* has also been reduced to fifteen minutes (*Aviation Report*, November 4, 1960).

[19] According to Press reports the *production cost* of a *Polaris* Fleet Ballistic Missile (FBM) is approximately $1 million. Original US Navy plans comprised the building of forty-five nuclear submarines at a unit cost of some

PLATE 3. Boeing *Minuteman* ICBM

[facing p. 34]

PLATE 4. Lockheed *Polaris* FBM.

more economical way, consistent with the geographical features of Western Europe. For example, the missiles could be installed on mobile submersible platforms and fired from random locations on the sea-bed, near the shore. The US technical Press alluded to a scheme which seems to be somewhat similar, designated *Project Hydra*; one thing appears certain—if the *Polaris* can be fired from tubes on board a submarine from a considerable depth, the same sequence of operations can be reproduced from an underwater pad near the coastline.

The firing controls and check-out equipment could be located on dry land, in direct communication by cable with the weapon on its submarine stand. Tactically such a deployment would be simple and, as mentioned above, the distribution and movement of weapons could follow a random pattern. If changes of location were also effected at random intervals, the enemy reconnaissance and intelligence organization would have a difficult task in pinpointing the instantaneous positions of the offshore launching pads. To add to the confusion, dummy platforms could be used, rendering the problem of identification more complex, even with the help of an orbital surveillance system.

Paradoxically, nations with limited defence budgets should pay particular attention to the latest trends in the field of more advanced strategic weapon systems. A closer and more imaginative evaluation might show that intermediate steps such as the ALBM should be omitted in favour of the next phase—for example, the mobile, not easily identifiable surface or under-water-launched ballistic missile. It must be remembered, however, that there is no such thing as the ultimate weapon and long-range ballistic missiles are simply the introductory phase of aerospace armaments proper. Therefore, even the poorer nations cannot afford to ignore these portents and assume that *Polaris*-class weapons will retain their deterrent validity in the 1970s.

$100 million. Research and development costs were estimated at about $2 billion (i.e. $2,000 million).

So far as British space policy is concerned, the first sign of a dawning realization of the importance of aerospace weapons was the establishment of a Deputy Directorate of Operational Requirements (Space) at the Air Ministry. Initially, it cannot be expected that such nascent interest will go beyond the feasibility studies stage; nevertheless it might well give a lead to other Western European NATO countries.

Finally, there are the first signs of activity in inter-Governmental and industrial circles in connection with the initiation of space research on a Western European scale. This will be discussed in more detail in Chapter IV.

CHAPTER III

Growth of Aerospace Technology

The indications are that aerospace weapons will constitute a *quantum jump* in armaments and methods of warfare, contrary to opinions voiced by various "experts" eager to dismiss orbital weapons as a form of space fiction. Earnest attempts are being made in USA and USSR to assess the true military potential of aerospace vehicles and devices, but this seems to have little tangible effect upon official thinking outside these two countries.

This *refusal to think* may have disastrous results. If the hypotheses on which the present essay is founded prove to be correct, USA and USSR will finally emerge as the only two World Powers capable of implementing global policies. Western European nations and the Red satellites would then sink to the status of "Roman auxiliaries", too weak to play a decisive part in world politics outside the sphere of Cold War and peripheral conflicts.

*

As defined earlier the term *aerospace* will be used to denote the technological and industrial fields of activity which comprise conventional aeronautics, ballistics and the simpler forms of orbital and space devices. We have also defined *astronautics* as the science and technology of locomotion outside the terrestrial atmosphere. Therefore, a review of aerospace can begin with some of the techniques derived from astronautics: this is simple

37

logic since future evolution will tend outwards into space, not back to the surface of the Earth.

The progress of astronautics has been extremely rapid, particularly if one remembers that the original mathematical treatment of space locomotion problems by Ziolkovsky was presented less than sixty years ago.[1] Since then the unprecedented rate of expansion of astronautics has given rise to what amounts to a new industry in USA. No doubt this industry has its counterpart in the Soviet Union.

Broadly speaking, astronautics is the combined result of two distinct trends of thought: firstly, the concept of the rocket as a weapon—starting with the Chinese fire arrows (*circa* A.D. 1200) and leading up to the German *V-2* of World War II; secondly, as the expression of man's ambition to penetrate into regions beyond the atmosphere of the Earth.[2] The present situation is that the more advanced military members of the aerospace family, e.g. Intercontinental Ballistic Missiles, are in fact the lowest form of non-aerodynamic vehicles. These weapons are also the *building blocks* for the first generation of experimental orbital and space devices.

To the uninformed the German *V-2* came as an unpleasant surprise. Early in 1944, only some six months before the impact of the first rocket in the London area, well-known scientists, e.g. the late Lord Cherwell, refused to consider the potentialities of such weapons. Post-war literature shows that even in Germany the military authorities were reluctant to give full support to the Peenemuende venture and only the pioneering zeal of Dr. Wernher von Braun, General Dornberger and of their colleagues ensured the successful completion of the very ambitious *V-2* programme. Actually, the German rocket technique reached such an advanced stage that after the war captured *V-2* rockets were used by the Americans for research purposes. It is a sobering thought that the *V-2* motor was in

---

[1] K. E. Ziolkovsky: *The Rocket in Cosmic Space*, in Russian, 1903.

[2] Oddly enough, Cyrano de Bergerac in his book *Le Voyage dans la Lune* (first half of seventeenth century), describes a three-stage vehicle, each stage consisting of six clustered rockets (*Science et Vie*, July 1961).

fact the basic prototype of power plants installed in current models of US ballistic weapons.

It has been said that the military regard scientific space research as a useful cover, whereas scientists look upon military enterprises as a convenient source of available hardware and cash. Scientific interests will be mentioned in the present book, but it is important to establish that one of the primary factors responsible for the unprecedented rate of development of aerospace science and technology was, and still is, the stimulus provided by their potential military applications.

*

As an introduction to the review of US military aerospace activities, a brief reference must be made to ballistic missiles which, apart from their value as weapons, constitute the *building blocks* of the early generations of aerospace and orbital vehicles and devices.

Immediately after World War II the German *V-2* became the virtual point of departure of the US aerospace research and development programme. In 1949 test firings of rockets captured in Germany culminated in the launching of a two-step assembly, with the *V-2* as booster, reaching an altitude of 242 miles. In parallel with *V-2* experiments, the US Armed Forces developed their own programme, including a number of research vehicles—for example the Martin *Viking*. At the same time a military programme was set in motion and the first coherent references to Intercontinental Ballistic Missiles appeared in the technical Press in 1954–55. Simultaneously, smaller ballistic weapons were being designed and developed; for instance, the short-range model by the Redstone Arsenal— which finally became known as *Jupiter*.

Eventually the various ballistic weapons separated into four distinct groups:

icbm—Intercontinental Ballistic Missiles with ranges of 5,000 miles or more.

irbm—Intermediate-Range Ballistic Missiles of somewhat

39

TABLE 2
US strategic ballistic missiles

| Missile | Prime contractor | Military designation | Lift-off weight (lb) | Dimensions (ft) | | Rocket motors (thrust in lb) | | | Maximum range (statute mile) |
				Length	Dia. (1st stage)	Booster	Sustainer or 2nd stage	3rd stage	
Atlas D* .	Convair	SM-65 (ICBM)	266,000	82.5	10	liquid 330,000	liquid 60,000	nil	9,200
Titan 1 .	Martin	SM-68A (ICBM)	220,000	98	10	liquid 300,000	liquid 80,000	nil	6,300
Titan 2† .	Martin	SM-68B (ICBM)	300,000	102	10	storable liquid 430,000	storable liquid 100,000	nil	10,000
Thor .	Douglas	SM-75 (IRBM)	110,000	65	8	liquid 150,000	nil	nil	1,700
Minuteman‡ .	Boeing	SM-80 (ICBM)	65,000	60	6	solid 160,000	solid ?	solid ?	6,300
Polaris A-1§ .	Lockheed	FBM	28,000	28	4.5	solid 100,000	?	nil	1,400

Guidance: Thor, Minuteman, Polaris and later models of Atlas and Titan—all-inertial.

* Atlas E—first successful launch: February 24, 1961; distance covered: 7,000 miles; total lift-off thrust: 390,000 lb.
† Titan 3—resembling the configuration of Titan 1 and 2: 200 ft long, will probably be used as space booster.
‡ It is reported that during 1965–70 the Minuteman will be replaced by the miniaturized Midgetman ICBM with a lift-off weight of 29,000 lb.
§ The improved Polaris A-3 to be derived from the test A-2 (30.5 ft in length, lift-off weight 30,000 lb) will carry an increased load of improved solid propellant. Early in 1961 an experimental A-2 covered 1,730 statute miles. The A-3 would have a range of 2,650 statute miles. Lockheed are also studying the A-4 with a range of 4,000 to 5,000 miles (Missiles and Rockets, August 21, 1961).

similar configuration, but with ranges of the order of 1,500 miles.

FBM—Fleet Ballistic Missiles, weapon systems specially designed for launching from submarines. The original range was of the order of 1,200 to 1,500 miles, but is to be increased to some 2,500 miles.

TBM—Tactical Ballistic Missiles, mainly as Army weapons, with ranges of a few hundred miles or less.

For obvious reasons no official information has been released with regard to the yields of warheads carried by the various ballistic missiles under development in USA. Unconfirmed statements and estimates have appeared in the technical Press but are not included in Table 2 giving the main characteristics of ballistic weapons which will constitute the principal ingredients of the US *bomber-missile mix*.

It may be of interest to give here an example of the influence which military requirements exert upon the design of the vehicles proper. The original Convair *Atlas* was to have a considerably higher lift-off weight and the rocket motors programmed for it were of larger size, possibly approaching the reported. booster ratings of the various *sputniks* and probes launched by the Soviets. However, in the course of the design of the *Atlas* it transpired that the fusion warhead could be made much smaller and lighter. As a result the vehicle was scaled down and the *SM-65 Atlas D* has a lift-off weight of 266,000 lb. This *Model D* is the first operational missile and has a smaller warload and a heavy copper nose-cone. The *E series* has a higher take-off thrust and weight; it is fitted with an ablation head which is lighter and carries a heavier charge. The *F series* will operate on non-cryogenic propellants.[3]

No special comments are needed in connection with Table 2, but one point of interest is the eventual replacement of the Convair *Atlas* and Martin *Titan* by the Boeing *Minuteman*.[4] The advantages of a solid-propellant weapon system are evi-

[3] *Aviation Report*, June 16, 1961.
[4] The first mobile *Minuteman* ICBM unit (the 4062nd Strategic Missile Wing, USAF) was activated in December 1960 (*Astronautics*, January 1961).

dent, particularly if it is to be installed in short count-down silo systems or on mobile platforms, e.g. railway trains. Incidentally, the basic design of the *Minuteman* is such that by removing one stage it could be converted into an IRBM and the top component used by itself could become a TBM.

There are indications that an attempt may be made to convert elements of the *Minuteman* into an ALBM (air-launched ballistic missile).

*

The first officially-announced space project in USA was the *Vanguard* satellite. The system, developed under the auspices of the US Navy for the International Geophysical Year,[5] was an essentially civil project. It was virtually unclassified and had very low priority—hence the delays and its tardy appearance in orbit, well after the launching of the first Russian *sputniks*.

Descriptions of various US satellites and probes have appeared in the technical Press and therefore it would be superfluous to review them in detail in the present essay, and only summaries are given in Table 21 (p. 124) and Table 23 (Appendix I, p. 138). This may not be quite consistent with the plan of the book, since this particular chapter is devoted to scientific and civil applications of astronautics. It was thought, however, that in the present state of development of orbitals and probes early military models could be regarded as experimental vehicles, closely related to the "scientific" class.

A truly significant launch—a "first" by US standards— was the ballistic "lob" achieved by Commander Allen B. Shepard, USN, who on May 5, 1961, performed the first US manned sub-orbital flight on board *Freedom 7*. The booster was a *Redstone* and the capsule designed in accordance with the *Mercury* programme.

The capsule reached an apogee of 115 miles, resulting in approximately five minutes of weightless state. After some eight minutes of flight, re-entry began and the drogue parachute opened at 21,000 ft. The capsule came down in the sea and

[5] July 1957–December 1958.

the astronaut was picked up by helicopter, the total duration of the flight being approximately fifteen minutes.

The astronaut suffered no ill effects, but it was reported that retardation at re-entry was of the order of 10g. An interesting point is that Commander Shepard used manual controls to test the effects of the pitch, yaw and roll jets.

On July 21 Captain V. Grissom, USAF, did a similar flight; the astronaut was picked up, but for undisclosed reasons the capsule sank before it could be recovered by helicopter.

*

In parallel with the *Vanguard*, the US Armed Forces—particularly the USAF—began to take active interest in the military aspects of aerospace work. The various projects envisaged and the vehicles built cannot be reviewed in detail, but the process was a gradual one, closely linked with the development of ballistic missiles. Thus, components borrowed from weapon programmes now constitute the building blocks incorporated in new aerospace systems.

At this point it may be preferable to define a few technical terms essential to the clear understanding of contemporary aerospace programmes. Thus, the components of the complete vehicle or device used for propulsion form the *carrier*. The carrier may consist of a number of stages or steps; the most important is the first or lower part, which is usually the largest, designed to lift the complete vehicle or device off the surface of the Earth and to accelerate it into a curved path towards higher altitudes. This lower component or stage, known as the *booster*, is jettisoned after *burn-out* and the next stage ignited, which further accelerates the remaining portion of the carrier with its payload. The next steps can be fired in sequence to put the vehicle into an orbit or achieve escape velocity, but in special instances—say, if the device is to be placed in a *parking orbit*—the stage may not be discarded and the motors are re-lit when the orbit is to be changed. The total number of steps will vary according to missions, but the significant feature of an aerospace system is its launching stage, i.e. the booster. It can be said that the latter determines the capabilities of the complete system.

The US programme is the best available example of a combined evolution of the more primitive orbital devices and ballistic weapons into a major aerospace plan. It can be conveniently subdivided into a number of phases or *generations*. Originally three generations were discussed in the technical Press, but the latest improvements and diversification of designs made these subdivisions obsolete. It is therefore preferable to use as a basis the classification put forward by Dr. Wernher von Braun in one of his papers.[6]

This information is summarized in Table 3 (pp. 46–7); it is important to note, however, that since the presentation of the paper important changes were made in the US space programme. The table has been brought up to date as far as possible, though some of the data published in the technical Press are somewhat vague and in some cases contradictory.

Tables 4 and 5 provide some additional information. The list of major NASA launchings may need correction if the recently-announced acceleration of *Man-in-Space* programmes can in fact be implemented.

The build-up of the US space programme will depend upon the rocket motors available: the size and performance of these units govern the evolution of the booster and carrier units and, consequently, of the complete vehicle systems or devices.

The total lift-off thrusts will exceed the million pound mark and one of the ways of achieving these high figures is to use a multiplicity of rocket motors assembled in the form of *clusters*. At the same time the unit ratings are increasing; a good illustration is a typical range of US liquid-oxygen/kerosene motors now in the design and development stage:

Rocketdyne *H-1*: 188,000 lb unit thrust.

Rocketdyne *E-1*: 360,000 lb unit thrust.

[6] "United States Space Carrier Vehicle Programme", paper presented by Dr. Wernher von Braun at the 11th International Astronautical Congress in Stockholm on August 16, 1960.

Rocketdyne *F-1*: 1,500,000 lb unit thrust.[7]

There is also a liquid-hydrogen/liquid-oxygen motor for the upper stages of the *Saturn*:

Rocketdyne *J-2*: 200,000 lb unit thrust.

Solid-propellant units in the 1,000k class are also being developed in parallel with the above-mentioned types.

Reverting to the vehicles illustrated in Table 3, the classification adopted follows a chronological order.

In the FIRST GENERATION, the *Vanguard* satellites were supplemented by three *Explorers* carried by *Juno 1*, derived from a weapon design known as *Jupiter C*. These systems are described as *minimum vehicles* owing to their restricted orbital payloads.

The SECOND GENERATION comprises the more advanced devices, but is also based on earlier weapon components such as *Juno 2* and *Thor*, with additional new stages, e.g. the *Agena*.

The INTERMEDIATE PHASE consists entirely of *Atlas* boosters with different payloads—*Score* and *Midas 2* satellites, plus the experimental *Mercury* test capsule. It must be emphasized, however, that the Intermediate Phase is an experimental subprogramme preparatory to the Third Generation of systems optimized from developed existing hardware.

In the THIRD GENERATION the simplest and cheapest vehicle is the solid-propellant *Scout* designed for use on missions requiring only light payloads. The *Thor Agena B* and *Atlas Agena B* are extrapolations from the Second Generation and Intermediate Phase, but with significantly increased payloads. Furthermore, their second-stage engines can be cut off and reignited in space, in accordance with programmed instructions. The *Atlas Centaur* is an even more powerful model and includes many refinements in design representing an advanced version of an *Atlas*-based system.[8] Taking maximum advantage of its

[7] The technical Press also use abbreviations such as the letter k (kilo) to represent 1,000 lb thrust. Thus, the Rocketdyne *F-1* rocket would be described as a 1,500k motor.

[8] Convair also proposed a 900,000-lb thrust *Atlas G* as a space booster. With a *Centaur* upper stage it would have a 4,000-lb payload capability. Development time: 2 years; cost: $85 million (*Aviation Daily*, Jan. 3, 1961).

high-energy propellant second stage, the *Atlas Centaur* can put heavy payloads into orbit around the Earth, on the Moon, or be used to launch planetary probes of increased size.

The FOURTH and FIFTH GENERATION shown in the table consist of the *Saturn* family of boosters and of the modular *Nova*. This includes *Project Apollo* as payloads, a progression of manned

TABLE

Evolution of US

1st Generation	2nd Generation	Intermediate (2nd/3rd)
CARRIERS: *Juno 1*, (*Jupiter C*) *Vanguard*	CARRIERS: *Juno 2* *Thor Agena A* Vehicle boost capacity: Low orbit 300 lb *Thor Delta* Vehicle boost capacity: Low orbit 500 lb *Thor* Able Star* (re-startable motor) Vehicle boost capacity: Low orbit 1,000 lb	CARRIERS: *Atlas Score* *Atlas Mercury* *Atlas Able* *Atlas Agena A*
MISSIONS: Early orbitals	MISSIONS: All operational, e.g. *Echo 1*, *Tiros 2*, *Explorer 10*, *Transit*.	MISSIONS: *Midas 2*, *Mercury* programme.

* The new *Thor DM-21* is shorter, lighter and has 10 per cent. more thrust.

† *Saturn C-2* may be discarded, as the minimum lunar *Apollo* specification calls for a boost capacity of 100,000 lb. First *Saturn* launch on Oct. 27, 1961.

vehicles to follow the now purely experimental *Mercury* programme.

The FIFTH GENERATION proper would comprise spacecraft capable of manned flights to the Moon. In its initial form *Project Nova* was a six-step vehicle with liquid-propellant motors, but it appears that the USAF are now developing a 2,000k to

3

aerospace systems

3rd Generation	4th Generation	5th Generation
CARRIERS:	CARRIERS:	CARRIERS:
Scout	*Saturn C-1* (2-stage)	Modular *Nova*
Vehicle boost capacity:	Vehicle boost capacity:	Vehicle boost capacity:
Low orbit 150 lb	Low orbit 20,000 lb	Low orbit 320,000 to
Atlas Agena B	Escape 5,000 lb	380,000 lb
Vehicle boost capacity:	*Saturn C-2* (3-stage)†	Escape 100,000 to
Low orbit 5,000 lb	Vehicle boost capacity:	140,000 lb
Escape 750 lb	Low orbit 45,000 lb	
Thor Agena B	Escape 15,000 lb	
Vehicle boost capacity:	*Saturn C-3* (3-stage)	
Low orbit 1,600 lb	Vehicle boost capacity:	
Atlas Centaur	Low orbit 100,000 lb	
Vehicle boost capacity:	Escape 38,000 lb	
Low orbit 8,500 lb		
Escape 2,500 lb		
Titan 3		
Advanced *DynaSoar* and		
Space Plane		
MISSIONS:	PROPOSED MISSIONS:	TYPICAL MISSION:
Vertical space probing,	Lunar soft-landing,	Return soft-landing
small and medium	return missions with	flight to the Moon,
orbitals, lunar- hard and	orbital refuelling.	without orbital
soft-landing vehicles and	Heavy satellites	refuelling. *Apollo C*
interplanetary probes.	including stations and	three-man spacecraft
Discoverer and *Nimbus*	tankers.	as payload.
programmes.		

Note: "Low orbit" is assumed to be around 300 miles. The vehicle boost capacities given are only typical figures and may vary considerably for different projects.

TABLE 4   *Vehicle payloads*

Mission	Payload requirements (lb)
ORBITAL:	
Geophysical, meteorological . . .	500 to 2,000
Astronomical observatory . . .	3,500 to 6,000
ESCAPE:	
Geophysics (highly elliptical orbits), hard lunar landing	500 to 1,500
Planet orbiter, soft lunar landing . .	2,000 to 3,500
Three-man circumlunar flight, moon surface exploration, planet probe . .	10,000 to 20,000
Manned lunar landing and return . .	100,000 to 200,000

TABLE 5   *Planned major NASA launchings*

Mission	Year*	Corrected, end 1960
First orbital flight of an astronaut; first launchings of *Centaur* vehicle and lunar impact vehicle	1961	?
First instrumented probe to the vicinity of Venus and/or Mars; first launching of a two-stage *Saturn* vehicle	1962	1962–1964
First launchings of unmanned vehicle for controlled landing on the moon and orbiting astronomical observatory . . .	1963–1964	?
First unmanned vehicle intended to circumnavigate the moon and return to Earth; first reconnaissance of Mars and/or Venus by an unmanned vehicle . . .	1964	?
First flight test of a nuclear second stage .	1965	1965–1967
First launching in a programme leading to manned flight around the moon and to a near-Earth space station . . .	1965–1967	1965–1970
Manned flight to a moon landing and return to Earth†	after 1970	1970(?)

* *Missiles and Rockets*, August 8, 1960.

† On May 26, 1961, President Kennedy said: "We are determined that this nation will continue to be a pioneer in this new frontier of space." Press reports suggested that USA will make a special effort to put a man on the moon by 1970 (*Daily Telegraph*, London, May 27, 1961).

3,000k solid-propellant rocket unit for an improved version of this vehicle.

There are other applications of the *Saturn* in the form of *orbital stations* and *tankers*. The latter may be needed to refuel heavy lunar vehicles: it is cheaper and simpler to lift a smaller vehicle from the surface of the Earth, refuel it in the orbit and then launch it on its lunar mission. To achieve the same payload with a similar performance by direct lift-off from the Earth, a much bigger and heavier system would be required.

The first four generations of US aerospace vehicles and devices described above can be regarded as an established programme. No doubt various amendments will be made to the plan in the course of execution; in addition, a major breakthrough in the propulsion field may impose fundamental changes, particularly in the heavy orbital and space vehicle class.

Table 7 (pp. 50–1) gives a more detailed summary of the various US satellites and probes planned over the next fifteen years. Naturally this can be only a guess-estimate, but it gives a reasonably clear idea of the magnitude of the technical and industrial effort required.

To complete the picture the corresponding numbers of boosters and upper stages were added up; these figures do not include any commercial satellites and the forty *Discoverers* are also omitted.

TABLE 6

BOOSTERS:		UPPER STAGES:	
Redstone	11	Mercury	25
Thor	177	Rover	19
Atlas	756	Agena B	708
Titan	27	Able	10
Saturn	45	Delta	10
Nova	20	Centaur	68
		Saturn S2, S4, S5	28

TABLE 7 *

	Booster	Upper stage	Payload (lb)	Orbit (miles)	Launches 1960–71	Launches 1971–75	Mission
Tiros	Thor	Able	270	450	5	0	Weather
Nimbus	Thor	Agena B	650	700	17	30	Weather
Aeros	Atlas	Centaur		23,000	18	15	24-hr orbit, weather
OAO	Atlas	Agena B	3,500	550	24	15	Observatory
EGO	Atlas	Agena B	1,000	150–60,000	36	15	Geophysical observatory
Pogo	Thor	Agena B	1,500	150–60,000	6	0	ditto
OSO	Thor	Delta	350	300	9	0	Solar observ.
Rift	Saturn S1	Rover	19,000	350	2	10	Nuclear drive
Moonshot	Atlas	Able		escape	11	0	Lunar probe
Mercury	Redstone	Mercury	2,400	120	14	0	Manned
Apollo	Atlas	Agena B	20,000	300	21	10	ditto
	Saturn S1	S4 S5	8,500	escape			3-man circumlunar
Ranger 1/2	Atlas	Agena B	700	escape	7	0	Interplanetary
Ranger 3/4/5	Atlas	Agena B	2,500	escape	3	0	Hard lunar landing

50

	Booster	Upper stage	Payload (lb)	Orbit (miles)	Launches 1960–71	Launches 1971–75	Mission
Surveyor	Atlas	Centaur	2,500	escape	26	0	Soft lunar landing
Prospector	Saturn S1	S2, S4, S5	2,500	escape	7	5	Soft lunar landing and return
Mariner	Atlas	{ Agena B / Centaur }	8,500	escape	8	15	Mars, Venus
Voyager	Saturn S1	S2, S4, S5		escape	7	5	Mars landing
Man-on-Moon	Nova		135,000	escape	5	15	
Echo	Thor	Delta	130	1,000	4	0	Passive communication
Rebound	Atlas	Agena B			76	0	ditto
Courier	Thor	Able Star	475	650	5	15	Repeater
Advent	Atlas	Agena B	600	23,300	14	40	24-hr repeater
Transit	Thor	Able Star	230	230–180	70	30	Polaris Navigation
Samos	Atlas	Agena B	4,000	250–300	95	40	Photo and recon.
Midas	Atlas	Agena B	5,000	300	93	30	IR detector
Saint	Atlas	Agena B	3,000	500	62	30	Satellite inspector
Bambi	Atlas	Agena B			48	30	Anti-ICBM
DynaSoar 1	Titan 2	Titan	5,000		17	10	Satelloid
DynaSoar 2	Saturn			60			

* Aviation Report, May 26, 1961.

At this point it seems advisable to say a few more words about manned vehicles. The first project, under the designation *Mercury*, is sufficiently well known not to call for a detailed description.

The follow-on, i.e. *Project Apollo*, is connected with the *Saturn* and *Nova* programmes. It is reported that it differs very considerably from the *Mercury*: the *Apollo* capsule will have some aerodynamic lift to simplify guidance problems on re-entry. Although the capsule will not be fitted with wings, this aerodynamic effect will widen the re-entry corridor from 3½ to 40 miles.

The time schedule has not been kept and *Project Mercury* is running late, well behind the launch programme of its Soviet counterpart. Twelve partial tests have been performed from September 9, 1959, to February 21, 1961, nine being successful. This was followed by two manned shots, i.e. Commander Shepard's and Captain Grissom's recent flights.

Designs of more immediate military interest are the *DynaSoar 1* and the *DynaSoar 2* which can be described as *satelloids*, vehicles that are not true orbiters. Their main function is to fly *antipodal* distances, at near-orbital altitudes, but without actually going into orbit. A further development of an aerodynamic, but truly orbital vehicle, is the *Aerospace Plane*. This is visualized as a hypersonic aircraft scooping air and storing it for feeding its rocket motors at orbital heights.

The principle of operation of the air-scooping craft is based on the idea of collecting air at great altitudes, compressing and liquefying it. The oxygen is then separated from the nitrogen and burnt with the liquid hydrogen loaded into the vehicle's tanks before take-off. By weight it takes eight times as much liquid oxygen as liquid hydrogen to form the correct propellant mixture and therefore the *Aerospace Plane* should take off at about half its upper atmosphere flight weight. After "scooping" the liquid oxygen content of the tanks could be from 80 to 88 per cent. of the total propellant load.

This type of vehicle should be able to take off from an ordinary runway, scoop in air in the upper atmosphere to take on a load of oxygen and then act as an orbital tanker and supply station for other vehicles. Alternatively it could proceed on its own mission—say, to a soft-landing on the Moon and return to an Earth orbit.

The complexity of the craft itself and of its sub-systems—both vehicle-borne and Earth-stationed—is such that it is estimated to be of an order of 100 to 1,000 times more difficult to implement than the World War II *Manhattan Project* which produced the first atom bomb. Thus, it is unlikely that the aerospace plane will make an early appearance, but the concept is interesting if only as an indication of future possibilities in the field of sustained manned operations in orbit and in space.

*

In parallel with the design and development of hardware in the form of major systems of the *Saturn* class, considerable work is being done in the field of advanced propulsion. Thus, attempts are being made to devise long-endurance power plants. The conventional chemically-fuelled rocket can produce very high thrusts, but owing to its high consumption the firing time is short. Entirely new "non-conventional" systems such as *ion* and *plasma jets* would give much lower thrusts, but the duration in space would be greatly increased—expressed in hours or days or even in months, instead of seconds or minutes.

One of the great problems is the supply of power for these electric drives and, incidentally, for auxiliary mechanisms and instruments. Direct conversion of heat into electricity is a very interesting line of research since the weight and bulk of conventional generating equipment is prohibitive for aerospace applications. Long-endurance low-thrust electric rockets are shown in Plate 12 as the cruising power plant of an Avco project.

Nuclear propulsion is also being investigated and the indications are that translunar space vehicles, particularly of the manned variety, will start from an Earth orbit and cruise on long-endurance atomic motors.

As a numerical example, it was estimated that a *Saturn C-2* with a nuclear stage having a reactor power of 3,000 to 4,000 MW would more than double the payload of the complete vehicle.

*

The overall trend of Soviet aerospace work is much less clearly defined, but sufficient information is available to form a general picture of the scientific and industrial effort deployed to achieve the series of satellite and probe launches begun with the *Sputnik 1* on October 4, 1957.

There is evidence that USSR clamped a security cover on rocket propulsion technology back in 1935—a time when, in UK, the British Interplanetary Society was only two years old and was looked upon as a gathering of space-fiction addicts.

After World War II the Soviets secured a considerable portion of German rocket facilities and conscripted a number of scientists. By now USSR must be spending at least as much as USA, but the cost of the Russian programme has never been disclosed. One of the Soviet delegates at the 10th International Astronautical Congress in London, when asked about the funding of the *sputniks*, was interpreted as having replied that he had never really thought about it, but supposed they must have cost a lot of money.

Before discussing USSR orbitals, a brief review of reported medium- and long-range missiles may be of interest. The information available is sketchy but sufficient to form a general picture of Russian ballistic armaments.

T-2 IRBM: Two-stage ballistic missile powered by rockets operating on alcohol and liquid-oxygen propellant. It is supposed to be approximately 100 ft long and to weigh about 60 tons. The range is estimated at 1,500 to 1,800 statute miles, carrying a nuclear warhead and guided by a radio-inertial system.

T-3 ICBM: This is the principal Soviet operational strategic missile—a three-stage liquid-propellant rocket system with a supposed range of some 8,000 statute miles. It carries a thermonuclear warhead, has a length of approximately 110 ft and a lift-off weight of about 85 tons. It is thought that the first series of *T-3* has been operational since 1959.

T-4 IRBM: Two-stage liquid-propellant rocket, 50 to 55 ft long and 6½ ft dia.; lift-off weight of the order of 35 tons. It is believed that the *T-4* can carry a 1,800-lb warhead over a distance of 1,000 statute miles.

T-4A: Reported boost-glide vehicle somewhat similar to the Boeing *DynaSoar*. Its nuclear warload is estimated at 3,100 lb.

Golem FBM: Estimated range about 400 miles; launched by submarine, but so far as it is known it can only be fired from the surface. There are reports of an experimental version of an underwater-launched *Golem* with a range of 1,250 statute miles.

*

Little reliable information is to be found in the technical Press on Russian missile and rocket motor programmes. After the *sputnik* and *lunik* launches more data were released, though still very sparse by US standards. Broadly speaking, Soviet policy is to disclose the results of the experiments but not the means of achieving these results.

The list of reported USSR ballistic missiles suggests that Russian designers have at their disposal a range of *building blocks*, at least as varied as those available in USA. Cluster assemblies, combined with a selection of more generously-sized rocket motors, no doubt helped the Soviets to speed-up the development of their vehicles and open the era of orbiters with the *Sputnik 1* well ahead of the Americans.

The Russians have gained a number of other important "firsts", e.g. animal (dog *Laika*) in orbit (*Sputnik 2*), artificial planet (*Lunik 1*), hard lunar landing (*Lunik 2*) and photographs of the far side of the Moon (*Lunik 3*). On August 20, 1960, the 4½-ton man-sized *Sputnik 5* was claimed to have successfully landed its capsule carrying two dogs, mice and other live specimens on its eighteenth orbital circuit of the Earth. On February 4, 1961, *Spaceship 4* was launched, weighing about 14,300 lb, the heaviest vehicle to be put into orbit at that date.

This was followed on February 12 by a *Venusian Probe* of some 1,000 lb launched from orbit by a *sputnik*.

The most important Soviet "first" was achieved on April 12, 1961, when the USSR Government announced that Major Y. Gagarin, on board satellite *Vostok*, had *gone into orbit* and, after one circuit of the Earth, effected a successful re-entry in a 4½-ton capsule. Undoubtedly this constitutes a major event in the history of astronautics; unfortunately the mystery surrounding this performance and the lack of official information on the technical characteristics of the vehicle detract from the scientific and technological value of this first manned orbital experiment. Doubts were expressed and questions asked— a natural reaction when compared with the very elaborate and open arrangements made by the Americans in connection with Commander Shepard's and Captain Grissom's flights.

Then, on August 6, 1961, *Vostok 2* went into orbit with Major Titov on board. This was a much longer flight of 25-hr 18-min duration, totalling seventeen orbits; apparently the capsule touch-down was by parachute, the occupant being ejected and landing separately.

We can now assume that the problems of manned lift-off and re-entry have been solved. While the multi-circuit orbital flight of August 6 is much more significant than the previous experiments, it is still unlikely to provide all the necessary data to assess the cumulative effects of the environment on a human being. In manned weapon systems it would be uneconomical to consider tours of duty in orbit of, say, less than a week; moreover, the average altitude at which Defence and Attack Platforms should operate is certainly higher, probably of the order of 500 miles.

It now seems that the problems remaining to be solved are not so much weightlessness as other environmental hazards[9]—

[9] Attempts are now being made to discover a probability pattern in sunspot activity with particular reference to manned space flight. The indications are that safe periods (without shielding) may be of short duration, i.e. a few days (*Missiles and Rockets*, August 7, 1961).

for example predictable and unpredictable radiation effects, the latter including solar flares.

*

Certain tentative conclusions may be drawn from reported Soviet aerospace activities:

1. USSR space carriers and boosters—so far as thrust and size are concerned and assuming Soviet industry to be working at the same rate as its American counterpart—were about three years ahead by mid-1960.

2. The payload capacity of Soviet orbital vehicles is greater than that of US models. This is illustrated in Fig. 4 and suggests a possible continuing divergence to the disadvantage of the Americans.

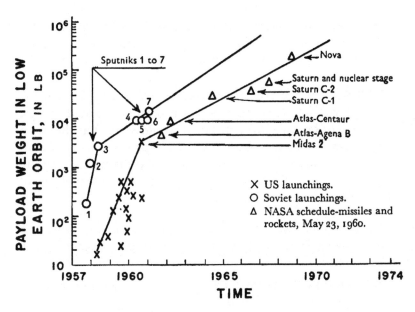

FIG. 4. Payload capacity of rockets (*Astronautics*, June 1961).

3. Guidance, judging by the *sputniks* and *luniks* as compared with the US satellites and probes, is at least on a par with USA.

4. The construction of early Russian satellites and instruments seems to be cruder than that of the Americans. Also there is little evidence of efficient miniaturization, there being an almost surprisingly small number of instruments when one considers the magnitude of the payload. It is probable, however, that this no longer applies, particularly in the more sophisticated vehicles such as *Sputnik 8*.

5. Political requirements seem to have had as much effect as scientific considerations. For example, more than 150 pieces of metal bearing the "Hammer and Sickle" were stowed in *Lunik 2* and scattered over the Moon's surface as a propaganda stunt. Whatever light alloy these were made of, they represented an appreciable dead weight which any scientist would have been only too glad to replace with instrumentation.

6. An evident objective of satellite and probe experimentation, apart from its importance in connection with weapon research, is to confirm the possibility of manned flight to the Moon.

7. Reports in the French technical Press suggested that some of the Soviet launches were performed from inclined ramps. This has not been confirmed, but it would seem that the main advantages of such a system would be improved accuracy and, possibly, a lower characteristic velocity. At the time of writing there was no confirmation of this alleged new technique in Russian technical literature.

Various unofficial forecasts have appeared in the Press and the following is an illustration of the supposed Soviet space programme:

Unmanned soft-landing on Moon . .	end 1961
Satellite rendezvous in orbit . . .	early 1962
Unmanned exploration vehicle landing on Moon	mid 1963
Manned circumnavigation of Moon . .	end 1963

Manned space station	. . . .	early 1965
Manned landing on Moon	. . .	mid 1967
Instrument landing on Venus or Mars .	.	mid 1968
Permanent orbiting station	. . .	early 1970

A comparison with dates shown in Table 5 suggests that the US programme is some three years behind. As stated previously, this is mainly due to the absence of high-thrust rocket motors: for instance, it is not expected that the flight qualification of the Rocketdyne *F-1* can be completed before 1963.

Thus, while the US space programme is mainly of a scientific and semi-experimental technological nature, the Soviet effort is directed towards *space flight*. Needless to say, the appearance of manned aerospace vehicles will have a decisive effect upon the design, mode of operation and military effectiveness of subsequent generations of orbital weapon systems.

＊

In the time scale of the present book a look into the more distant future would be of academic interest only; therefore it will be sufficient to indicate, in very general terms, the probable scale and hypothetical timing of astronautical programmes in the 1970s to 1990s.

At present the US *Nova* is the largest known practical project. No doubt the Soviets have its counterpart, since their programme includes manned travel to the Moon, obviously calling for vehicles with capabilities similar to those of the American "Fifth Generation".

In the present state of the art these large vehicles rely on a conventional form of propulsion, i.e. chemical rockets. Nuclear power plants must soon appear on the scene, first as auxiliary units and later as motors—in some instances in combination with long-duration electric rockets.

Eventually, total lift-off thrusts will be expressed in thousands of tons and entirely new types of motors will have to be considered, based, for instance, on the idea of *capsulated nuclear*

59

propulsion. This new theoretical concept is mentioned in Chapter V and is also shown as the last item in Table 8.

TABLE 8

Payloads and propulsion systems of future space vehicles
(According to *Aviation Report*, February 10, 1961)

System	Possible date	Escape payload (in 1,000 lb)	Main propulsion system
Saturn . . .	1965	15	Chemical rockets
Nova and "5th Generation" .	1970	100 to 200	ditto
Helios . . .	1975	250	Nuclear heat-exchange and electric rockets
Urania . . .	1980	500	ditto
Orion . . .	1990	1,300	Nuclear capsulated

The progression of payloads is sufficiently striking to need no further comment. The hypothetical *Orion* (see Plate 11, facing p. 115), with its escape payload of some 600 tons, belongs to the era of true spaceships.

CHAPTER IV

Industry and Budgets

World War I demonstrated the necessity for systematic research, design, development and production of aircraft. This
led to the creation of an entirely new industry, but early in life
it was not very robust and could only exist on military orders.
Consequently, soon after the end of World War I, a major
crisis arose and some of the aeroplane constructors disappeared,
others had to contract. In Britain, with a few exceptions, sur-
vivors had to vegetate on a very limited number of orders for
a depleted RAF.

A similar process of retrenchment and readjustment took
place in USA. A number of firms were compelled to take interest
in air transport and this helped the American aircraft industry
not only to survive the inter-war period, but to secure a strong
position in civil aviation.

The British aircraft industry revived when rearmament
began in 1936. A great effort was made to get new aircraft
models into quick production; a system of *shadow factories*
accelerated the expansion and peak productivity was reached
in 1941–42.

In USA the reactivation of military aircraft production was
much slower, in fact initiated by "cash-and-carry" contracts
placed by the British and French Governments. The further,
almost explosive expansion of the US industry—particularly
after Pearl Harbour—now belongs to history, but in the post-
World-War-II era events did not follow the pattern of 1920–40.

The unstable political equilibrium after 1945 and the

introduction of nuclear weapons as a constituent part of the armoury of the major Powers, prevented a wholesale slump in the military aircraft market. While production commitments were cut, the technological evolution of the airframe, power plant and accessories helped to maintain a reasonable level of expenditure on research and development.

In 1950 the Korean "peripheral incident" gave a fresh impetus to air armament work in Britain and USA, but after the termination of the war policies began to diverge. H.M. Government, in pursuit of a policy of economy, cut down research and development expenditure, thus slowing down the growth of new ideas and techniques.

A more cautious attitude prevailed in USA: the Pentagon clearly understood that research and development was an essential part of the defence policy and that new weapons such as guided missiles would assume a much greater importance than suggested by the strategically-indifferent outcome of the German *V-2* experiment. Eventually it was realized that orbital vehicles and devices were closely related to the heavy ballistic weapons; eventually the two programmes would overlap and time and money could be saved by using missile hardware in aerospace work.

From a limited number of concerns employing less than 100,000 throughout the world in the early 1930s, the aircraft industries in the various countries now provide a living for some 2½ million men and women. About 20 per cent. are on work connected with civil air transport, the balance being represented by the armament side of the industry. This evidently sharpens the latter's response to political and military events and considerable fluctuations in employment figures from one year to another have been recorded. On the other hand, the overall cut-back in production after World War II, to less than a fifth of the peak wartime output, persisted in the American and British industries until the onset of the Korean War.

The world's aircraft industry reached its peak strength in 1944, with a labour force of over 8 million. USA, Britain and

USSR contributed roughly 2 million each, Germany and Japan probably 1 million each. During World War II the Americans built some 300,000 military aircraft, the British 125,000 and the Germans around 110,000. No reliable figures are available for the other belligerents, but it can be assumed that both the Japanese and the Soviets each built at least 100,000 aircraft.

*

One distinguishing feature of the present period is the diversification of interests within the industry. Many new firms are now being drawn into the field of aerospace work, including electronics, navigational instruments and ground support equipment.

For instance, a survey performed by *Aviation Week* [1] revealed that the percentage of aircraft avionic engineers engaged on design and development within the US companies has doubled in the last five years. In 1954 only one-third of the industry's avionic technicians were doing "in house" design and development, with the balance employed on monitoring developments by outside contractors, installation work and flight-testing instrumentation. In 1959 two-thirds were engaged in "in house" design and development, with only one-third monitoring outside work or performing installation engineering and flight-testing instrumentation.

Table 9 shows the changing make-up of the technical staff employed by the US aircraft industry, now known as the *Aerospace Industry*. Thus, it is estimated that in 1964 the percentage of electrical and electronic engineers related to the total number of technicians will have doubled, i.e. from 18 per cent. in 1954.

According to statistics compiled by the Electronics Industries Association, military spending on missile electronics alone totalled $273 million in the first quarter of FY 1958. Intended primarily to depict trends, and subject to later revision, the EIA computation in Table 10 shows the following figures for

[1] *Aviation Week*, October 5, 1959.

the first quarters of Financial Years 1955–58, all ending September 30.[2]

TABLE 9   *Number of technicians in the US Aerospace Industry*

	Numbers			Approx. percentage of totals		
	1954	*1959*	*1964 (est.)*	*1954*	*1959*	*1964 (est.)*
Aero and mechanical	27,800	46,196	54,138	82	76	65
Electrical . .	6,200	14,728	28,719	18	24	35
Totals . .	34,000	60,924	82,857	100	100	100

TABLE 10

Budget category	First quarter FY 1955 ($ million)	First quarter FY 1956 ($ million)	First quarter FY 1957 ($ million)	First quarter FY 1958 ($ million)
Aircraft . .	238	299	213	340
Ships, harbour craft . .	19	17	17	23
Combat vehicles .	15	26	2	1
Support vehicles .	3	1	—	1
Missiles . .	59	115	205	273
Electrical and communication	145	168	130	204
R. & D. . .	56	60	65	73
Miscellaneous .	15	10	5	11
Totals	550	696	637	926

It is outside the scope of the present essay to go into a detailed study of the overall industrial situation, but a couple of examples may be of interest. Taking as an instance propellant requirements, these have been summarized in Table 11.

A new subsidiary branch of the aerospace industry is made up of firms specializing in the design, development and produc-

[2] *Missiles and Rockets*, February 1958.

TABLE II

Propellant requirements

	Thrust (million lb)	Availability dates	Propellant required (million lb)
ICBM	0.3	now	0.2
Saturn	1.5	1961–62	1
Nova	6.0	1968–70	4.15
Future	20.0	1972–75	14

tion of *ground support equipment* (GSE) for ballistic missiles and space vehicles and devices. This comprises test installations, launching pads, gantries, transporters and other ancillary equipment.

Typical space GSE covers research and experimental facilities and is exemplified by General Electric's range of activities:

1. SPACE LABORATORIES: most of the design features and actual equipment for experimental space laboratories (excluding the launch vehicle) will be developed with the help of specialists in the fields of optics, information data processing, sensors, etc. GSE engineers' main job is to integrate the equipment with the vehicle design and package it for the space environment.

2. SPACE ASSEMBLY: General Electric are working on the design of tools, assemblies, fixtures, shelters, etc., for space operations, including landings and travel on the Moon, planets and in deep space.

3. SPACE LOGISTICS AND MAINTENANCE: the work in this area covers supply plans for routine and emergency operations, maintenance procedures, fuel reserve and supply storage, ferry-transport scheduling and rendezvous, in-flight check-out and repair, etc.

The magnitude of missile GSE expenditure, as compared with aircraft, is illustrated in Table 12. This gives a clue to the cost of more sophisticated space GSE.

According to the Deputy Chief of Staff Material, the USAF

TABLE 12

Representative USAF figures

(*Space/Aeronautics*, October 1960)

Weapon system	GSE *expenditure in $ million*	
	FY *1960*	FY *1961*
AIRCRAFT:		
Boeing *B-52* Bomber	66.5	31.3
Republic *F-105* Fighter-bomber	33.7	29.9
MISSILES:		
Atlas ICBM	242.2	341.3
Titan ICBM	106.8	245.0
Minuteman ICBM	2.3	48.8
Hound Dog A-to-S missile	56.6	49.1

needed $802 million for missile GSE and a further $760 million for ground communication equipment.

So far as the US Navy is concerned, the GSE total for 1961 amounted to $434 million.

*

Reverting to the make-up of the aerospace industry proper, the preponderance of large firms or groups is an evident trend of evolution.

Aerospace and electronics continue to dominate the list of the top 100 defence suppliers who secured three-quarters of the $21.6 billion of military prime contracts awarded in 1960.

The list includes sixty-one companies responsible for research, development and production of aircraft, missiles or electronics. There are seven new companies in this category on the 1960 roster; eight aerospace and electronics concerns which were on the 1959 top 100 list failed to win enough contracts to be included in 1960.

The top 100 companies' share of total contracts rose from 74 per cent. in 1958 and 73.2 per cent. in 1959 to 74.6 per cent. last year. This increase is partly due to mergers and take-overs which consolidated the defence business of several firms. The 1960 list of top contractors is given in Table 13.

TABLE 13

One hundred top US contractors, 1960
(*Aviation Week*, July 3, 1961)

No.	Companies	Millions of dollars	Percentage of total
1	General Dynamics . . .	1,294.7	6.0
2	Lockheed Aircraft . . .	1,124.3	5.2
3	North American Aviation . .	964.1	4.4
4	General Electric	944.7	4.4
5	Boeing Co.	867.1	4.0
6	United Aircraft	739.1	3.4
7	Martin Co. . . .	708.4	3.3
8	AT & T	501.9	2.3
9	Hughes Aircraft	437.6	2.0
10	Raytheon Co.	374.2	1.8
11	RCA	364.8	1.7
12	Douglas Aircraft . . .	353.5	1.6
13	Grumman Aircraft . . .	336.6	1.5
14	Republic Aviation . . .	323.3	1.5
15	Sperry-Rand Corp. . . .	318.0	1.5
16	International Business Machines Corp.	312.1	1.4
17	Newport News Ship Building & Dry Dock	302.4	1.4
18	Bendix Corp	274.3	1.3
19	Westinghouse Electric . . .	269.5	1.3
20	General Tire & Rubber . .	257.8	1.1
21	General Motors Corp. . .	214.0	1.0
22	Chrysler Corp. . . .	199.5	1.0
23	Avco Corp. . . .	193.2	0.9
24	IT & T	188.3	0.8
25	Standard Oil Co. (New Jersey) .	163.7	0.8
26	Northrop Corp. . .	158.0	0.7
27	Thiokol Chemical . .	140.1	0.6
28	Burroughs Corp. . .	122.7	0.6
29	Chance Vought . . .	120.6	0.6
30	Hercules Powder . . .	118.8	0.5
31	McDonnell Aircraft . .	118.8	0.5
32	Pan American World Airways .	109.1	0.5
33	Philco Corp.	101.4	0.5
34	Thompson Ramo Wooldridge .	100.9	0.5
35	Collins Radio Co. . . .	99.0	0.4
36	Standard Oil Co. of California .	96.9	0.4

TABLE 13. *One hundred top US contractors, 1960—continued*

No.	*Companies*	*Millions of dollars*	*Percentage of total*
37	Minneapolis-Honeywell Regulator Co.	84.3	0.4
38	American Machine and Foundry Co.	83.9	0.4
39	General Precision Equipment Corp.	83.0	0.4
40	American Bosch Arma . . .	82.4	0.4
41	MIT	80.9	0.4
42	Garrett Corp. . . .	80.8	0.4
43	Textron	78.1	0.4
44	Ling-Temco Electronics .	76.9	0.3
45	Kaiser-Raymond-Macco-Puget Sound	75.4	0.3
46	Texaco	74.3	0.3
47	Curtiss-Wright Corp. . .	67.1	0.3
48	Goodyear Tire & Rubber Co. .	64.3	0.3
49	Food Machinery & Chemical Corp.	62.6	0.3
50	Continental Motors . .	62.4	0.3
51	Ryan Aeronautical Co.. .	56.2	0.3
52	Du Pont de Nemours & Co. .	55.4	0.3
53	Olin Mathieson Chemical Corp. .	53.4	0.3
54	Kiewit	52.7	0.3
55	General Telephone & Electronics Corp.	52.6	0.2
56	Shell Caribbean Petroleum Co. .	51.7	0.2
57	Merritt-Chapman & Scott Corp. .	49.2	0.2
58	Laboratory for Electronics .	48.9	0.2
59	Socony Mobil Oil Co. . .	47.1	0.2
60	Marquardt Corp. . .	46.3	0.2
61	Bethlehem Steel . . .	45.3	0.2
62	Lear	43.7	0.2
63	Magnavox Co. . . .	43.5	0.2
64	Northern Pump Co. . .	43.1	0.2
65	Mason & Hanger-Silas Mason Co.	42.6	0.2
66	Sanders Associates . . .	41.9	0.2
67	Todd Shipyards . . .	40.0	0.2
68	Motorola	38.0	0.2
69	Kaman Aircraft . . .	36.5	0.2
70	Ford Motor Co. . . .	36.2	0.2
71	Ingalls Iron Works Co.. .	35.0	0.2
72	Richfield Oil Corp. . .	34.1	0.2
73	System Development . .	32.8	0.2

TABLE 13. *One hundred top US contractors, 1960—continued*

No.	Companies	Millions of dollars	Percentage of total
74	Union Carbide Corp. . . .	32.0	0.2
75	Universal American . . .	31.3	0.2
76	Fairchild Engine & Airplane Corp.	30.8	0.2
77	Continental Oil Co. (Delaware) .	29.9	0.2
78	Goodrich (B. F.) Co. . . .	29.9	0.2
79	Standard Oil Co. (Indiana) . .	29.5	0.1
80	Gulf Oil Corp.	29.5	0.1
81	Firestone Tire & Rubber Co. .	29.4	0.1
82	International Harvester Co. . .	29.0	0.1
83	Vitro Corp. of America . .	28.7	0.1
84	Gilfillan Bros.	28.6	0.1
85	Cook Electric Co. . . .	28.3	0.1
86	Air Products . . .	27.8	0.1
87	Sinclair Oil.	27.8	0.1
88	Jones-Teter-Winkelman . .	27.8	0.1
89	Johns Hopkins University . .	27.7	0.1
90	Utah-Manhattan-Sundt . .	27.3	0.1
91	Litton Industries	27.2	0.1
92	Hallicrafters Co. . . .	26.9	0.1
93	Cities Service Co. . . .	26.2	0.1
94	Morrison-Knudsen Co.. . .	26.1	0.1
95	States Marine Corp. . . .	26.0	0.1
96	A R O, Inc.	25.9	0.1
97	Hazeltine Corp.	25.0	0.1
98	Union Oil Co. of California . .	24.6	0.1
99	Western Contracting . . .	24.2	0.1
100	Sunray Mid-Continent Oil Co. .	24.1	0.1

To be fully effective, research and development work must be planned and directed in an orderly and systematic fashion. While programming on a national scale is the responsibility of the appropriate government departments, aerospace firms must have their own evaluation and operational research facilities. In some cases a unit specially organized for the job has to be built up, to help the management in policy making, at the same time putting forward suggestions and ideas to the Armed Forces on subjects which have not been fully investigated by government agencies.

The industrial importance of *forward-thinking units* was clearly demonstrated by the recent changes in larger US concerns and the appearance of organizations specializing in this type of work. In addition, the US Government and constructors often use universities and other learned bodies as advisers and consultants, particularly in the more abstruse scientific fields. The growth in number and size of special bodies dealing with evaluation, advanced systems analysis, planning of research and of systems engineering, technical direction and monitoring of space systems has raised the total of such work to $110–120 million a year.

On the whole it is somewhat difficult to describe exactly the work of these special bodies, except by saying it is unique and highly sophisticated. Thus under the general heading of "Development Support" one finds an array of firms such as RAND, Aerospace Corporation, MITRE, ANSER, STL (Space Technology Laboratories), Lincoln Laboratory, etc. As far as individual 1962 budgets are concerned, RAND is to receive $11.6 million, STL $34.8 million, MITRE $15 million and the Lincoln Laboratory $15.3 million.[2a]

"In house" forward thinking, evaluation, operational research etc. are now a recognized necessity among the major US aerospace firms. For instance, in 1957 General Electric assembled a staff of more than fifty scientists and engineers to work on questions of vital importance both to the nation and to the Company. At the time the Company's Technical Military Planning Unit, called TEMPO, was unique in many respects in the US Defence Industry. Since then the idea has been spreading and other constructors have followed General Electric's lead.[3]

Another example of systematic advanced thinking fostered by private industry is the Research Institute for Advanced Studies (RIAS), a division of the Martin Co., USA, concerned exclusively with *basic research*, as distinct from so-called *applied research*. RIAS has no programme schedules in the industrial

[2a] *Aviation Report*, September 11, 1961.
[3] *Aviation Week*, October 14, 1957.

sense of the word; it deals only with fundamental disciplines such as mathematics, physics, biology, chemistry and metallurgy. The Parent Company claim that in the RIAS Mathematics Centre they have the largest group of mathematicians in the Free World devoted to the study of non-linear differential equations. The Biosciences Group of the Institute is engaged in an intensive study of photosynthesis, the life-sustaining process by which plants produce food. When RIAS began to function, contracts from Government agencies covered only 5 per cent. of its annual costs; in 1960 they covered more than 40 per cent.

The following quotations from an address given in 1960 by Mr. William B. Bergen (President of the Martin Co.), before the New York Society of Security Analysts, define the distinctive features of the new aerospace industry:

". . . World War II was won, essentially, on *quantity* of weaponry. All present indications are that, if there is a World War III, it will be won by whichever side possesses at the *outset* weaponry of superior *quality*, though probably in very small quantities, indeed, compared to World War II's fleets of combat planes. For this reason the nature of defence contractors' products today bears little resemblance to those of World War II.

"There are fewer and fewer production lines of the type we had in the past. On the other hand, there is more and more research and development in a never-ending effort to turn out better and still better weapon systems. It is no longer sufficient to stay on a par with your potential enemy; the only safe way is to stay at least one step ahead of him to ensure national survival. And, quite clearly, a second-best could be worse than no defence at all. . . ."

*

The preceding discussion should give a general idea of the evolution of the aircraft industry—in fact its transmutation into an aerospace complex. It will be interesting to see how this is reflected in military expenditure; for example, in US budgets.

TABLE 14

Missile and aircraft procurement Fiscal Year 1962

(*Missiles and Rockets*, June 5, 1961)

Service	Funds authorized, $ Million			
	Aircraft total	Missile total	Typical allocations in missile budget	Remarks
USAF . .	4,101.1	2,792.0	Atlas SM-65 : 201.6 Titan SM-68 : 1,129.8 Minuteman SM-80 : 923.8 Ballistic Missile Support: 180	Diverted to R.,D.,T. & E.: 73.5 ditto 356.4 ditto 377.0
US Navy . . .	1,677.8	644.4	Polaris : 354.4	R.,D.,T. & E. (Additional) : 443.2
US Army . . .	211.0	550.8	Anti-tank and ballistic missiles	Including Nike-Zeus anti-ICBM
Totals . .	5,989.9	3,987.2		
Grand Total . .	9,977.1			

(R., D., T. & E.: Research, development, test and evaluation.)

Striking evidence of the accelerating trend of development away from manned aircraft towards missiles is provided by the fact that, whereas in 1954 USAF were spending about 90 per cent. of their budget on aircraft and only 10 per cent. on missiles, the percentage of total procurement money spent on missiles and astronautics had risen in 1960 to nearly 34 per cent. of the total air and aerospace procurement of the three Services.

Mention was made in Chapter II of a possible increase of missile programme reaching a total of over 3,900 in Financial Year 1967. The cost of such programmes would amount to $12.5 billion for the fixed *Minuteman*, $2.9 billion for mobile *Minuteman*, $3.1 billion for the *Titan* and $8.6 billion for the *Polaris*. Incidentally, the scale of forward planning by USAF is illustrated by the growing complexity of Systems Command. Its organization was fully described in the US Technical Press[3a] and all that need be said here is that in 1962 this Command will spend $7 billion; in years to come it will have an aggregate budget of some $60 billion covering the full cycle of development and production of weapon systems now under its control.

Such a long-term view must necessarily reflect in the Fiscal Year 1962 budget. The original Eisenhower budget for FY 1961 included over $10 billion for missile and aerospace work; additional proposals were laid before the Kennedy administration in January 1961 to increase this budget by $2 to $4 billion. Since then several further adjustments have been made, bringing the total US defence budget to $46.8 billion.

Table 14 shows the totals of missile and aircraft procurement for FY 1962. It illustrates the importance of the *Titan*, *Minuteman* and *Polaris*, bearing in mind the significant switch of portions of some of the production budgets to research, development, test and evaluation. The *Polaris* has its own separate R., D., T. & E. budget shown under "Remarks" in Table 14. The grand total of these allocations is very nearly $10 billion.

[3a] Special issue of *Aviation Week and Space Technology*, September 25, 1961.

TABLE 15

USAF Research, Development, Test and Evaluation Programme

	($ million)		
	FY 1961	FY 1962	Remarks
Atlas ICBM	4.6	1.0	Strategic weapon systems
Titan ICBM . . .	3.3	2.0	
Minuteman ICBM . . .	4.2	3.5	
Skybolt ALBM . . .	111.1	89.0	
Samos satellite . . .	273.8	276.0	
Midas satellite . . .	107.4	201.0	Defence system
Advanced development, including Discoverer and Blue Scout orbiters, DynaSoar boost-glider, tri-service Fighter . .	386.0	406.7	
Applied research . .	243.3	266.9	
Basic research . . .	42.1	52.5	
Other items . . .	593.0	633.3	Including civilian personnel and contractor-operated installations
Total . . .	1768.8	1931.9	

Note: additional R., D., T. & E. funds for the *Atlas, Titan* and *Minuteman* will be diverted from Procurement (see Table 14).

Table 15 gives the list of funds to be assigned by USAF alone to research, development, test and evaluation of missiles and space devices. Again certain items stand out by the amounts allocated or by increases over FY 1961 figures. For instance, *Midas* satellite funds have been nearly doubled; also, additional money will go to other aerospace and orbital vehicles and to applied research.

NASA budgets are quite distinct from those of the Armed Forces; there again the total increase has been considerable, namely from $1,109 million to $1,784 million. The budgetary breakdown is shown in Table 16, and attention must be drawn to Project *Apollo*. This has been increased from $29.5 million in the original January 1961 plan to the revised figure (May 1961) of $160 million. The *DynaSoar* may get an additional $85 million out of USAF funds to speed up the sub-orbital flight programme by six months.

The *Saturn* booster, which, in a way, is the keystone of the US space programme, has also benefited by an increase from $168 million to $224 million. Another interesting point is that $48½ million have been assigned to Project *Nova*, plus $28

TABLE 16

FY 1962 NASA budgets

| | $ million | | |
	Original (*Jan. 1961*)	Revised (*May 1961*)	*Remarks* (M = million)
R. & D.:			
Support of NASA plant .	74.3	89.1	
Scientific satellites . .	64.7	72.7	
Lunar and planetary .	103.9	159.9	
Meteorological satellites .	28.2	50.2	
Communications satellites	34.6	94.6	
Project *Mercury* . .	74.2	74.2	
Project *Apollo* . .	29.5	160.0	
Propulsion . . .	78.6	102.9	Including electric: $6.8 M
Nuclear systems . .	24.0	36.0	
Boosters . . .	205.6	287.2	*Saturn* from $168 to $224 M
Project *Nova* . . .	—	48.5	
Other items . . .	102.2	120.2	
Total R. & D. .	819.8	1295.5	
Construction . . .	99.8	262.1	Including $28 M for *Nova* launch facilities
Personnel . . .	190.0	226.7	Personnel increase from 17,300 to 21,400
Grand Total .	1109.6	1784.3	

million for its launch facilities. This Project did not appear in the original January 1961 estimates; therefore it is obvious that the decision to expedite *Man-in-Space* and lunar plans, in direct competition with USSR, is reflected in these major schemes.[4]

*

While a certain amount of non-systematized information is available on the costs of missile and space systems, an accurate analysis of figures, related to budgets, presents very considerable if not insuperable difficulties. Various attempts have been made to compute the average costs per lb of payload, per lb of lift-off weight, etc., but the results thus obtained do not appear to be reliable and will not be quoted.

Nevertheless, Table 17 was prepared to provide a yardstick of approximate costs of aerospace systems under development in USA. The unit costs are more in the nature of guess-estimates since it is virtually impossible to correlate with any degree of accuracy the published research and development (R. & D.) and production figures in missile and aerospace budgets.[5] Later information shows, however, that these costs may be much higher: Table 18 includes development costs of the first series of vehicles—nine in the case of the *Scout* and ten for the *Centaur* and *Saturn*.[6]

An interesting evaluation of future trends of spending was made by Dr. Murray L. Weidenbaum (Boeing Aeroplane Co.), predicting a steady rise of US Department of Defense budgets to nearly $49 billion by 1970.[7] Obviously all such forecasts must be based on a number of assumptions: for instance, that Cold War will continue and that there will be no major disarmament agreement between West and East.

[4] *Missiles and Rockets*, June 5, 1961.
[5] *Aviation Report*, May 27, 1960; *Aviation Week*, July 4, 1960; *Missiles and Rockets*, November 7, 1960; *Aviation Week*, April 3, 1961, etc.
[6] *Missiles and Rockets*, March 6, 1961.
[7] *Missiles and Rockets*, November 14, 1960. Since the publication of the article the total FY 1962 budget rose to $46.8 billion.

TABLE 17

Individual system costs.

System	Estimated unit cost ($ million)	Up to mid-1960	Actual and possible allocations in $ million				
			FY 1961	FY 1962	FY 1963	FY 1964	FY 1965
BOOSTERS:							
Centaur	9.1	41.0	53.1	56.4			
Delta	2.6	26.3	11.8	2.9			
Saturn	17.3		118.1	224.2	↕ 100 to 200 ↑		
Blue Scout		8.8	5.6	15.0			
Scout	0.75		4.0	3.7			
PAYLOADS AND PROJECTS:							
Saint			6.1	26.0			
Advent		97.5	100.0	160.0	20	150 to 200 ↑	↑
Apollo							
Discoverer		⎰	273.8	276.0			
Samos	6.7	⎱ 988.6	107.4	201.0			
Midas		⎰	58.0	185.0			
DynaSoar		125.5					
Explorer							
Mariner				10 to 20			
Mercury	6.4	251.5	109.5	74.2		50 to 70 ↑	↑
Pioneer				10 to 20			
Prospector		9.8					
Rover		61.0	10.0	50.0			
Shepherd							
Space Plane				20.0			
Tiros	14.5			48.5			
Transit		33.0		7.0			
Nova							
North American X-15		141.0	6.0				

Note: blank spaces in table indicate absence of information; figures between arrows are possible yearly levels.

77

TABLE 18

Costs, including development

Vehicle	Cost per vehicle	Cost per operational launch
	($ million)	
Scout . .	1.79	0.94
Centaur . .	17 to 18	7.5
Saturn C-1 .	100	20

The figures given in the Boeing analysis were summarized and replotted in Fig. 5. The top line shows the total yearly military expenditure, one two-cycle log scale being used to facilitate the reading of partial totals.

The lines showing expenditure on aircraft, missiles and astronautics come under the heading of *procurement only*, i.e. do not include basic research costs, maintenance, etc. R. & D. costs are shown separately, but comprise the whole range of armaments, not only aircraft and guided weapons. An approximation was given, namely that about one-fourth of military R. & D. funds is devoted to *research*; the balance of 75 per cent. is spent on the *development* of weapon systems. The amount devoted to *basic research* comes to a little over $100 million a year.

NASA were responsible for the scientific investigation of space for civil applications and therefore their budgets should be treated separately. From $500 million in 1960 the NASA total would go up to about $1.75 billion in 1964, levelling off between 1967 and 1970 at some $2.1 billion per year.[8] This is shown by a simple broken line in Fig. 5.

[8] The original FY 1962 budget totalled $1.1 billion in January 1961; in May it was increased to nearly $1.8 billion (Table 16). It is also reported that the FY 1963 NASA total may go up to $4 billion, more than half of this sum being intended for lunar projects (*Missiles and Rockets*, August 21, 1961).

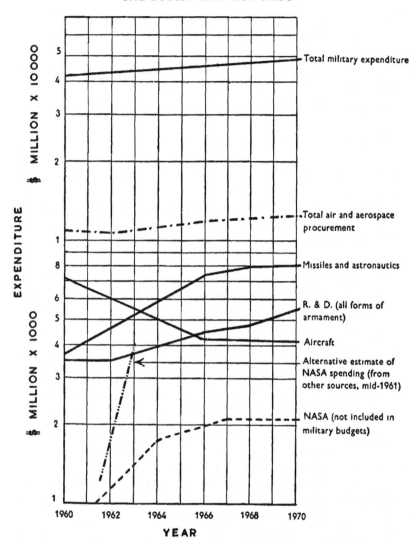

FIG. 5. Forecast of expenditure.

Finally, it is worth noting that the missile and astronautics expenditure and the cost of aircraft procurement should be about equal in 1963. The cross-over would occur at a figure of $5.5 billion, giving a total of some $11 billion for military

79

procurement in the missile, astronautics and aircraft field.

To conclude, the Weidenbaum forecasts seem to have already been overtaken by events. Nevertheless, the overall trends illustrated in Fig. 5 probably remain valid, particularly as an illustration of the "cross-over" of aircraft and missile-astronautics spending.

*

The position in Western Europe is different inasmuch as Governments appear to be mainly concerned with the preservation of the economic equilibrium of their respective countries. Only major political upheavals seem likely to produce a reaction and result in a renewal of interest in advanced armament design and development.

The discrepancy in military spending between USA and other NATO countries is illustrated in Table 19, showing the respective defence expenditures.

It is important to note, however, that these figures represent the total defence costs, i.e. air and surface forces combined.

Such is the position in the conventional aircraft field; in more advanced aerospace and orbital work the discrepancy is overwhelming, in fact it is improbable that any one of the Western European Powers, including Britain, can implement a significant aerospace programme of its own.

While the apportioning of military production contracts between various countries is a feasible proposition, confirmed by one or two reasonably successful instances in the history of NATO, the co-ordination of advanced research and development is a much more complex problem. It may well be that the only possible solution would be a Western European system of collaboration on an *industrial* basis, covering research and development together with civil and scientific applications of aerospace technology. The activities of government departments would then be limited to general supervision, administration of national budgets and the working out of overall requirements and specifications.

TABLE 19

Total defence costs

	Expenditure in $ million			1959 expenditure per head of population in $
	1957	1958	1959	
USA . . .	44,380.0	45,528.0	47,315.0	300.2
Canada . .	1,869.0	1,804.6	1,888.3	121.0
France . .	3,712.8	3,939.6	4,275.6	97.4
UK . . .	4,390.4	5,577.6	4,510.8	88.2
W. Germany .	2,133.6	1,629.6	2,744.0	54.3
Belgium . .	367.4	367.9	394.0	44.2
Norway . .	146.7	143.4	151.5	43.4
Turkey . .	475.9	530.0	785.7	37.5
Netherlands .	486.9	438.2	403.2	37.0
Denmark . .	146.4	143.4	149.0	33.0
Luxemburg .	8.7	8.7	7.8	26.0
Greece . .	149.2	149.0	163.0	20.2
Italy . . .	977.5	1,035.2	1,019.2	18.8
Portugal . .	83.7	86.8	93.0	10.1
Total Europe .	13,078.2	12,929.3	14,696.6	55.2
Total N. America	46,249.3	47,332.6	48,203.1	283.6

Various official attempts are now being made to establish a joint European programme of space research. Actually these efforts do not convey the impression of an orderly plan and it is suspected that some of the arrangements which are being sought or made are in the nature of compromises and expedients. Naturally this is better than no programme at all, but it remains to be seen whether any real *entente* can be arrived at between the Western European countries on such an insecure basis.

As matters stand at present there are two main organizations seeking to establish contact between governmental departments and agencies. The first one is the European Space Research Organization (ESRO) and the second the proposed European Space Launcher Organization (ESLO) or European Launcher Development Organization (ELDO); the latter is to be based on the utilization of the *Blue Streak*, which is no longer supported by H.M. Government as part of the UK weapon programme.

In the writer's opinion there is a distinct danger that the various European countries will be tempted to establish their own space programmes and thus weaken a potential joint effort. A French space budget is already in existence and there are reports of a German budget, only part of which will be allocated to ESRO and ELDO.

Probably a more hopeful sign is the tendency of certain Western European industrial firms to get together to study the possibilities of aerospace research and development. The first attempt to evaluate some of the commercial and military aspects of the problem was the Report issued by Hawker Siddeley Aviation Limited (UK) and the Société pour l'Etude et la Réalisation d'Engins Balistiques (France).[9]

*

The question of how much Western Europe can afford to spend on a space programme is a vexed one. Various guesses have been made, but it is now quite obvious that no single country, acting independently, can make a significant contribution to the technological competition between the "Big U" Powers.

It is probable that the various Governments involved in the ESLO and ESRO plans have worked out some sort of budgets, but for the purpose of the present study it is logical to take a more independent assessment based on a straightforward analysis of the situation in USA and Western Europe. An example of such a study can be found in Chapter II of the Hawker Siddeley-SEREB Report mentioned above.

The evaluation begins with a review of USA spending over the Fiscal Years 1958, 1959, 1960 and 1961: the overall space budgets over these four years make a total of $3.2 billion.

[9] *Industry and Space.* Report issued by Hawker Siddeley Aviation Limited (UK) and SEREB (France) in February 1961.

The general trend of the Report can be illustrated by quotations:

". . . The American space effort has up to now constituted 2 to 3 per cent. of the defence effort. While it is true that the development and speeding up of the programme has been announced, it may be assumed that a large part of the increase will be derived from transferring allocations from other sections of the budget.

"Such an effort, while reasonable for the US, is beyond the reach of Western Europe and even more so of any single European nation. In order to determine the scale of the European effort weighting factors have been introduced to take account both of gross national product and of the proportions set aside by the European countries for defence, in relation to this gross income. This method, however arbitrary, is well known to the NATO countries and enables an idea to be gained of the limits of the effort which could be envisaged. . . ."

A table given in the Report analyses the total defence expenditure in relation to the gross national product and shows the following ratios:

". . . About 10 per cent. for USA.
About 7 per cent. for UK and France.
About 5 per cent. for other Western European
countries.

"This leads to the conclusion that the relative effort of France and Britain is 70 per cent. of the American one, while the Western European effort is only 50 per cent. Furthermore, the proportion of the European gross national product in comparison to that of the US is shown to be about 25 per cent. for the UK and France combined and 50 per cent. for all OEEC countries . . ."

". . . While America has devoted $3,200 million to space activities in the past four years, the various European associations should be able to muster over a four-year period a total sum, which could be, according to assumptions made, as follows:

"—About $400 to $560 million, were Britain and France to collaborate either in such a manner that their contributions reach the average European level or such that their effort would be about the same as that allocated by the two countries for defence.

"—About $800 to $1,100 million for all the member-countries of OEEC dependent on whether an average of 50 per cent. or a more ambitious 70 per cent. of the American effort is assumed. . . ."

". . . In order to estimate the European cost of European projects, account has been taken of the differing price levels between the two continents (European cost = 60 per cent. of the US cost). . . ."

". . . An evaluation on these lines leads to a breakdown of expenditure for a European programme approximately as follows:

Research, equipment, data acquisition and handling	$300 million
Technological developments (including vehicles)	$300 million
Specific space applications . . .	$200 million
Total . .	$800 million

"This total alone demonstrates the value of co-operation in as wide a European framework as possible. The association of certain British Commonwealth countries, as, for example, Australia and Canada, would further enable either the scale of the programme to be increased or the financial burden of the countries concerned to be proportionately reduced. . . ."

Thus, the figure of $800 million spread over four years is a good indication of what Western Europe could do if an earnest attempt were made to organize a combined effort, with a realistic and effective programme.

This total of $800 million spread *equally* over four years, and limited only to European countries belonging to NATO, would represent a yearly expenditure per head of population of 81 US cents, i.e. 5*s*. 10*d*.[10] These figures speak for themselves and are very modest compared to US spending. Taking the NASA budgets alone, without the hardware supplied from military programmes, the corresponding American yearly spending is of the order of $10 (£3. 11*s*. 6*d*.) per inhabitant.

*

The Hawker Siddeley-SEREB Report appears to have initiated a new trend of thought among European industrialists and, as a result, an association has been formed under the name of EUROSPACE. This is a non-profit-making organization, and one of its tasks is the study and evaluation of aerospace projects and techniques, supplemented by planning of work on a Western European scale. Collaboration with US constructors is also envisaged, especially in the advanced research field. The latter may be an important part of the whole scheme since it is to be expected that the American industry will be under heavy pressure in the technological race now in progress with USSR. The "brain potential" of Western Europe is very considerable and it is mainly a matter of efficient organization to achieve a co-ordination of advanced research capacity on both sides of the Atlantic. A practical and effective system of collaboration in this field is more likely to be built up on an industrial level, with a minimum of governmental interference.

*

It is extremely difficult to assess the magnitude of USSR budgets, but a well-documented study was published in an American technical journal,[11] based on data collected from the Western European specialist press.

Table 20 consists of official Soviet figures ("National Total")

[10] According to the *1961–62 Civil Estimates* (Ministry of Aviation, Class VI, Vote 9), "work by Industry, etc. in aid of space research satellites" is costed at £4 million. This represents about 1*s*. 7*d*. per head of population.
[11] *Missiles and Rockets*, June 20, 1960.

and results of evaluations and analyses by the author of the Article ("Actual military funds" and "Rocket and space research"). Budgets in roubles cannot be converted directly into dollars or pounds since the rate of exchange varied from $1 = 4 old roubles (official) to $1 = 15 old roubles (black market).[12] Therefore the significant figures are the percentages of the national total, the latter being taken as 100 per cent. for each particular year.

TABLE 20

USSR military budgets

	Budgets (in billions of old roubles)			
	1957	*1958*	*1959*	*1960 (est.)*
National Total . . .	603.8	627.7	707.6	744.8
Actual military funds . .	209.8	213.5	225.4	267.1
Rocket and space research .	27.6	28.1	28.3	39.5

	Ratios (%)			
	1957	*1958*	*1959*	*1960 (est.)*
National Total . . .	100.0	100.0	100.0	100.0
Actual military funds . .	34.7	34.0	31.8	35.8
Rocket and space research .	4.6	4.5	4.0	5.3

To relate these allocations of funds to the actual strength of Soviet armed forces, the 1960 total defence budget of 267.1 billion old roubles included the maintenance of a labour force of 200,000 on rocket production and a planned deployment of 165 missile bases. Therefore the 39.5 billion old roubles in the same column seem to represent only a part of the USSR investment in missile and aerospace science and technology.

[12] The new rouble equals 10 old roubles. Official rate: $1 = 0.9 NR.

CHAPTER V

Further Evolution of Aerospace Weapons

━━━━━━━━━

As a preamble to the discussion of the probable pattern of evolution of aerospace weapon systems, mention should be made of President Eisenhower's speech at the United Nations plenary session on September 22, 1960.

Addressing the Assembly, the President appealed for disarmament and made a special reference to orbital weapons. On the issue of outer space he proposed that all launchings of spacecraft should be checked in advance by UN. Subject to appropriate verifications, no nation would put weapons of mass destruction into orbit or station them in outer space.

A statement of this importance made at one of the crucial meetings of UN, in the presence of Mr. Khrushchev and of his associates, suggests a certain anxiety with regard to the potentialities of space armaments. It confirms the deductions made from the study of the technical Press, namely that military operations will tend to spread into orbital space as the logical extrapolation of the strategic ballistic missile.

A former official British scientist was reported to have said that *"there can be no military reason for getting into space"*[1]; in other words that the American effort to build up an aerospace force is—to say the least of it—misguided. Everyone is entitled to his own opinions, but in the field of aerospace research, development and construction USA have acquired a great deal of experience, and co-related strategic thinking is

[1] *Aviation Report*, January 27, 1961.

immeasurably more advanced [1a] than the immediate-post-World-War-II mentality still predominant in Western Europe.

Therefore it is relevant to reproduce here two extracts from statements made by responsible US officials, a striking contrast with the sample of primitive thinking quoted earlier.

On April 11, 1961, Air Force Secretary Eugene M. Zuckert told the Senate Armed Services Committee that "the United States and the Free World must insure that the means of Earth domination inherent in space mastery be not pre-empted by the enemies of Freedom. . . . The lesson is that through and from space Earth can be dominated."

The same day General Thomas White also addressed the Committee:

". . . The Soviets could launch a large space platform—truly a major rung in the ladder of the achievement of effective space weapons systems. There also are many indications that they may put a man into space within the very near future."

The USSR manned vehicle *Vostok 1* went into orbit on the following day.

*

As described in Chapter II, the present phase is that of transition from strategic bombing aircraft to strategic ballistic weapons. While the proportion of manned aeroplanes will diminish in relation to ballistic missiles, it does not mean that manned bombers will disappear from air force inventories before the end of the present decade. Even if they lose most of their effectiveness as massive retaliation systems, supersonic aircraft of the North American *B-70* type may have to be used against pinpoint objectives—for example, mobile targets or in cases when target map co-ordinates are not accurately known.

Current technological trends point to a gradual evolution of strategic ballistic missiles into orbital weapons. This process will probably go through a number of connecting links, one of

[1a] For instance the report by Dr. Walter Dornberger on *Military Utilization of Space* (*Aviation Week and Space Technology*, September 18, 1961).

which may be some form of *Delayed Impact Space Missile*. The simplest DISM would be a non-orbiting weapon with a very different path from that of a conventional ICBM. This represents considerable advantages, since the detection and interception of, say, "spiralling" devices, could be made more difficult by programmed deviations from the normal trajectory, combined with a very high arrival velocity. It is thought that with the accuracy and weight of *Lunik 2* and *Lunik 3*, the Soviets could send up missiles along such paths reaching out several thousand miles into space, confusing by decoys their identification by defence bases in New England, Greenland and Alaska.

The principal characteristic of the DISM's performance is the time margin available after the launch. This is a highly important feature, since a critical decision could be involved in the initiation of reprisal procedures against an enemy missile attack on a warning lacking incontrovertible confirmation. The conventional ICBM takes only a short time to reach its target, and the final interpretation of, say, radar plots may reveal an error, so that a global conflagration could be brought about by a technical mistake. The advantage of the DISM is that it can be *destructed* [2] after some delay, should an error have occurred; the longer transit time of a DISM-type weapon allows a greater margin for a decision to be taken with a reasonable knowledge of circumstances and of the enemy's intentions.

A considerable number of USAF space projects has been mentioned in the technical Press, but the following classes of military systems—planned or under development—give a broad idea of the expanded space programme:

OFFENSIVE

1. *Positive Control Bombardment System* (*Recallable* ICBM) consisting of three-ton nuclear-armed satellites in 100-mile orbits.[3] Part of general category of advanced weapon system studies grouped under System Requirement (SR) 199.

[2] Deliberate destruction of a missile by the launching station.
[3] Each *jump-down satellite* would be within range of its appointed target for eighteen minutes during each circuit of the Earth and would be triggered by radio command (*The Aeroplane and Astronautics*, February 3, 1961).

DEFENSIVE

2. *Project* SPAD (Satellite Protection for Area Defence): early warning anti-ICBM orbital, eventually an anti-ICBM system. This designation has become a generic description of any anti-ICBM weapon employing satellite techniques.

3. *Random Barrage* (RBS): 20,000 to 100,000 satellites in random orbits, the device itself making the kill. It is also intended as an anti-ICBM defence system.

4. *Project Saint:* programme of orbitals with interception,

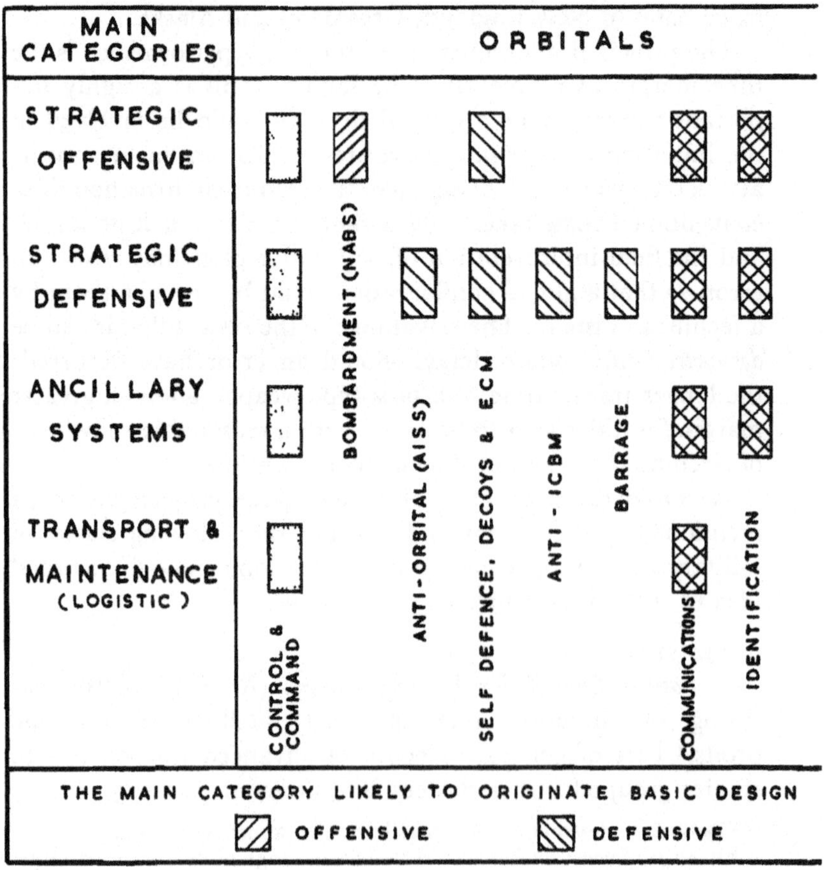

MAIN CATEGORIES	ORBITALS						
STRATEGIC OFFENSIVE							
STRATEGIC DEFENSIVE							
ANCILLARY SYSTEMS							
TRANSPORT & MAINTENANCE (LOGISTIC)	CONTROL & COMMAND	BOMBARDMENT (NABS)	ANTI-ORBITAL (AISS)	SELF DEFENCE, DECOYS & ECM	ANTI-ICBM	BARRAGE	COMMUNICATIONS / IDENTIFICATION

THE MAIN CATEGORY LIKELY TO ORIGINATE BASIC DESIGN

OFFENSIVE   DEFENSIVE

FIG. 6. Classification of

inspection and kill capabilities against unidentified and/or hostile satellites.

5. *Project* INSATRAC: a development and follow-on of *Saint*.

LOGISTIC

6. *Project* SLOMAR: a space logistic, maintenance and rescue programme.

7. *Project* SMART: satellite maintenance and repair.

8. *Project Phoenix:* military space-launching system.

orbital weapon systems.

RECONNAISSANCE

9 and 10. *Samos* and *Midas* orbitals.

COMMUNICATION

11. *Project Csar:* advanced research stationary satellite.

One difficulty is to devise a reasonably simple classification of various forms of space weapons. In many instances the technical characteristics of defensive, offensive, ancillary and logistic systems tend to overlap and Fig. 6 is an illustration of this complex relationship. It will be seen that the same basic orbital designs may meet several categories of military applications.

At this stage of the discussion the differences between manned and unmanned orbital systems may be ignored, but it is evident that the eventual appearance of *platforms*, operated by specially selected and trained crews, will greatly improve the flexibility and effectiveness of aerospace weapons.

OFFENSIVE WEAPONS

The first strategic attack systems will lie in an intermediate area where both aerodynamic and ballistic régimes come into play. An example, already mentioned, is the boost-glider—for instance the Boeing *DynaSoar*.[4] The idea is not a new one and is derived from Professor E. Sänger's original scheme, consisting of a hypersonic aircraft with ballistic flight phases.

Concurrently, there are reports of a Soviet hypersonic boost-glide vehicle which is supposed to be near its flight development stage. This is the *T-4A* mentioned in Chapter III.

We have already mentioned the existence of a new project —the *Space Plane*. This of course is a very ambitious undertaking and the reported flight-test programme in 1962–68 appears to be very optimistic. Nevertheless, it points to an eventual replacement of the Boeing *DynaSoar* [5] by a manned vehicle, with a flight weight in excess of 500,000 lb.

[4] Phase 1 *DynaSoar*: glider weighing 9,000 to 10,000 lb, with *Titan J* booster; total lift-off weight 242,000 lb (*Missiles and Rockets*, Sept. 26, 1960).

[5] The *DynaSoar sub-orbital* programme may eventually be eliminated; using a *Saturn* booster this vehicle could become *orbital*, resulting in a time saving of 2½ years (*Aviation Week and Space Technology*, August 14, 1961).

Thus the connecting link between the conventional ICBM and future attack satellites will probably be the DISM or its development, the low-altitude bomber-orbiter—the *Recallable* ICBM. The technical Press has reported this trend and referred to USAF Requirement SR-79821.[6] From the military point of view there may be certain similarities with the Boeing *DynaSoar* and two types are mentioned—one for deployment up to a 20,000 nautical miles range and the other, described as *Strategic High-Altitude Orbital Bomber*, with operational capability in excess of that figure.

The feasibility and military potential of *Nuclear-armed Bombardment Satellites* (NABS) with higher orbits and longer life have been evaluated by the USAF. At present opinions are divided, but concern over possible Soviet work in this direction may speed up the USAF Satellite Interceptor Programme exemplified by Project *Saint*.[7]

The first argument in favour of NABS is that an orbital device is virtually the ultimate in mobility and a powerful psychological deterrent or "weapon of dissuasion". Secondly, underground or underwater-sited ballistic missiles may gradually lose some of their deterrent value, particularly when public opinion becomes accustomed to threats and counter-threats by invisible and conceivably non-existent weapons. A bombardment satellite in orbit can be a permanent reminder of retaliatory power in being. Thirdly, orbit-changing NABS would be far less vulnerable to surprise attack. While it is theoretically possible to destroy such a vehicle, anti-satellite operations would give warning of a possible generalized nuclear onslaught.

On the negative side is the interception risk of a fixed-orbit satellite. Therefore, attack systems with programmed or tele-controlled variable orbits must be envisaged, or else weapons monitored by manned orbital platforms. This is confirmed by USAF support of several parallel studies of later-generation

[6] *Aviation Week*, December 26, 1960.
[7] A pointer to Soviet interest in orbital weapons was Major-General T. I. Pokrovsky's reference to bombardment satellites in an article published shortly before the launching of *Sputnik 1*.

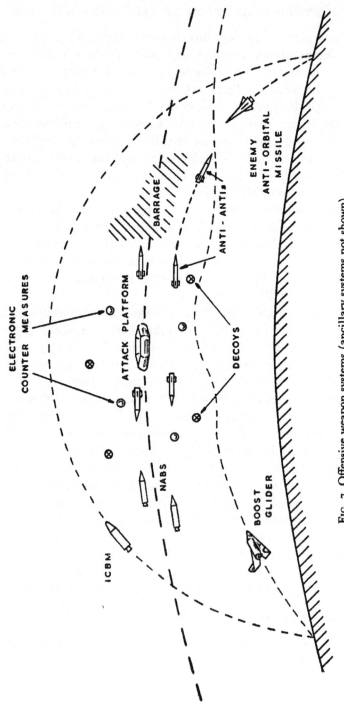

FIG. 7. Offensive weapon systems (ancillary systems not shown).

satellites capable of manœuvring to avoid interception by hostile vehicles.[8] A further drawback is that unmanned weapon systems cannot be given a complete operational check-out in space and faults corrected before release. Therefore the array of unmonitored NABs to be placed in orbit would be several times the number of surface-launched ICBMs required to perform a given mission.

Evidently these are very strong arguments against the programmed or surface-controlled NABs, but objections would be greatly weakened when manned or space-monitored orbital systems become practicable. Project SMART may well be an attempt to overcome this inherent defect of "parked" space weapons.

Another argument put forward against a bombardment satellite force is that in the event of an orbital conflict the losing side would still retain its surface reprisal capability in the form of ICBMs and submarine-launched weapons. This may be so, but a point to remember is that the present-day deterrent weapon concept would have to be re-evaluated if a virtually automatic "second wave" nuclear attack from space, in response to the reprisal salvo, were to finish off the defending side. The corollary is that a complete system of defence must comprise both NABs and anti-orbitals.

From the military point of view manned vehicles have considerable advantages, but their deployment would necessitate the establishment of a very complex organization. An attack platform could be operated by a crew of two or three doing a limited tour of duty in orbit, the change-over being effected at regular intervals by ferry rockets. The configuration and size of such an orbital is still indeterminate, but it seems that the rotating wheel form is satisfactory in providing an artificial gravity environment.

An attack platform with some of its associated systems is illustrated in Fig. 7.

The weapons proper, circulating in their own orbits, can be released and directed by the manned platform, the types and

[8] *Aviation Week*, October 24, 1960.

missions varying from NABS to anti-orbitals and anti-ICBM devices. Guidance of these weapons will pose a number of very arduous problems, but the strategic reward is worth the effort. One of the obvious targets of monitored NABS would be naval vessels and sea transport in general. Whereas even a slow ship can avoid an ICBM due to the time required for feeding in the information and for count-down, an evasion manœuvre from a NABS monitored by an attack platform may not be possible because of the short count-down and the different method of guidance.

As stated previously, manned platforms and satellite stations must be of the variable orbit type, in order to avoid counter-attacks by space defence systems.

Satellite stations would be supplemented by special systems for defence against anti-orbital weapons of the enemy. These would consist of special orbiting weapons controlled by the attack platforms and which could be directed against enemy missiles or orbitals—which means that these devices must have orbit-changing and close-approach capability.

An example of passive defence is a counter-orbiting belt of artificial meteorites which can be loosely compared to mine-fields in surface warfare. Bumper shields would have to be used to protect the orbital vehicles circulating in or crossing these danger zones. Somewhat similar belts of micro-dipoles, on the lines of Project *Needles*,[9] could be used to confuse enemy observation and warning systems.

The systems described would be supplemented by active ECM (*Electronic Counter-measures*) decoys with special radar or infra-red response characteristics simulating full-scale orbiters or weapons.

DEFENSIVE WEAPONS

As mentioned previously, it is difficult to draw a purely technical line of demarcation between offensive and defensive systems. Both classes of weapons must have means of self-

[9] One billion (10^9) micro-dipoles, weighing about 220 lb, could create a signal-reflecting belt (*Aviation Week*, September 19, 1960). Later re-named *Westford*.

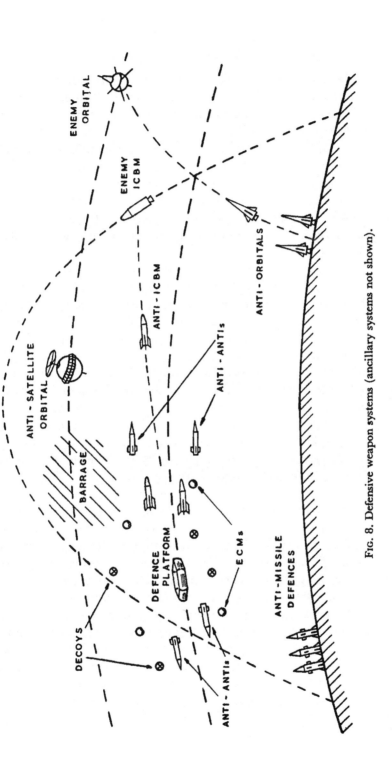

FIG. 8. Defensive weapon systems (ancillary systems not shown).

protection, but the strategic defence organization would have one characteristic feature—the inclusion of anti-ICBM armament operating in conjunction with recce, early warning, surveillance and inspection satellites.

An orbital anti-ICBM defence system is evidently of very great importance and no doubt every effort will be made to include these weapons in the strategic space defence organization of the major Powers. As indicated in the introductory part of the present chapter, US planning comprises Project SPAD and the *Random Barrage*—both being accorded considerable attention.

The feasibility of a satellite-based ICBM defence system is now being evaluated by Convair, Hughes Aircraft and Space Technology Laboratories, the work being sponsored by the Defence Department's ARPA as part of Project *Defender*.[10]

A satellite-based ICBM system, similar to the original Project *Bambi* (Ballistic Missile Booster Interceptor) would require between 800 to 3,600 satellites in low-altitude orbits to provide full global coverage. An important part of this concept is the interception of ballistic missiles during the ascent phase, when the boosters are easily detected by their infra-red radiation. Also, a kill during the boost period presents an advantage since it gives little or no opportunity to the enemy to launch decoys at this early phase of the flight.

The system envisaged includes the requirement that the satellite launch platforms must be within several hundred miles of hostile missile pads or silos. It remains to be seen whether USSR—or USA for that matter—would tolerate the presence of armed anti-ICBM satellites over their territories, even if the intercepting devices carried non-nuclear warheads.

While this plan of intercepting ICBMs from orbit is in its early theoretical stage, it is interesting to note that some of its advantages are already becoming manifest. In fact it might well prove to be the only satisfactory way of destroying ICBMs in flight, apart from entirely new and novel methods involving the use of, say, electric pulses, "slugs" of plasma, etc.

[10] *Aviation Week and Space Technology*, October 23, 1961.

PLATE 5. Boeing *DynaSoar* (left).

PLATE 6 *Midas 3* satellite with *Agena B* stage (right).

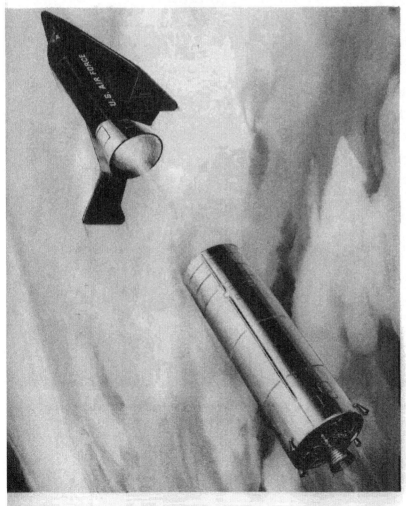

PLATE 7
Vostok
capsule.

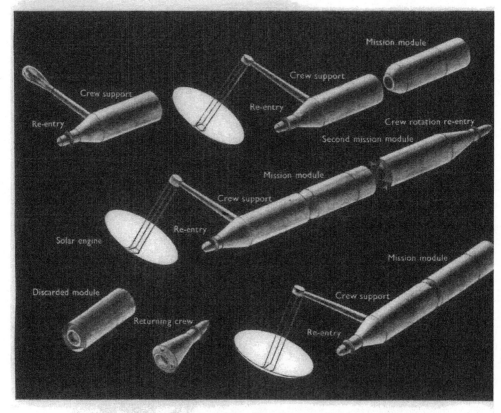

PLATE 8. Martin Project *Deimos* (Development and Investigation of a
Military Orbital System). This artist's conception shows sequence of *Deimos*
system from rendezvous and closing of first crew and mission module (top)
through stages of crew replacement.

[facing p. 99]

There is no need to dwell upon the strategic importance of devising an effective system of anti-ICBM defence since it would deprive the side defeated in orbit of any further means of effective surface retaliation against its victorious opponent.

Strategic defence weapons against orbitals fall into two classes: firstly, devices circulating in orbit, automatic or monitored by manned platforms—the former type exemplified by the Westinghouse project mentioned in the technical Press[11]; secondly, weapons launched from the ground or an aircraft in flight.

A circulating orbit-changing device will become an essential requirement against hostile variable-path orbitals. An example is US Project *Saint* anti-satellite orbital, which corresponds to a reported USAF programme for a *rendezvous* device with close-approach capability. The design and development of such a vehicle is a major undertaking, but it is considered that its equipment with infra-red and nuclear sensors is relatively easy. The same applies to providing the anti-satellite with the required *kill capability*.

Project *Saint* (now *Satellite Inspection Technique* instead of original *Satellite Interception Technique*) is divided into inspection and destruction phases. One of the difficulties is to discriminate between decoys and genuine warloads and between scientific and military payloads; so far the most promising method seems to be the measurement of the satellite's mass with small mass-indicating decoy. More than twenty experimental vehicles will be required for this programme, probably made up of *Atlas* and *Agena B* steps.

A more advanced form of defence organization is illustrated in Fig. 8. This presupposes the existence of manned defence platforms monitoring and controlling the anti-satellite and anti-ICBM armament. Interdiction belts, artificial meteorites and decoys would complete this comprehensive defence system.

The ground- or air-launched weapon would be mainly effective against fixed-orbit targets or vehicles with restricted orbit-changing capability—in fact the first phase of develop-

[11] *The Aeroplane and Astronautics*, October 7, 1960.

ment of anti-space armament. Technically speaking it is important to distinguish between two main variants, namely:

1. A device launched from the ground, directed to intercept the enemy satellite in its orbit. The weapon would probably be equipped with an appropriate type of sensing device or proximity fuze.

2. A device launched from an aircraft in flight, otherwise similar to the surface-based version. While guidance requirements are more complex, there are advantages in the reduction of booster size and improved pre-launch mobility of the weapon.

The feasibility of the latter type of weapon was demonstrated on October 13, 1959, when the Martin *Bold Orion* experimental Air-Launched Ballistic Missile was fired from a Boeing *B-47* bomber towards a point ten miles ahead of *Explorer 6*. Although *Bold Orion* was not initially designed as an anti-orbital weapon, it suggests that the USAF have under active consideration the use of ALBMs against enemy satellites.

Little is known about the warheads of anti-orbital devices, but presumably nuclear charges would be employed.[12] In space the blast is nil, but the thermal effect and radiation flux can damage or neutralize orbital vehicles and devices. Radiation alone can put out of action some of the essential electronic equipment of a satellite.

A more detailed review of the technical Press shows that these problems are being studied and a rough idea can be obtained of the probable effectiveness of atomic explosions in vacuum, directed against unmanned vehicles and devices. In the absence of blast effect, thermal radiation and neutron flux assume a particular importance: Rand Corporation's formula gives an indication of the lethality of a nuclear deflagration in space:

$$R = 4200(P/d^2),$$

where R = flux in röntgens (r), P = yield in kilotons (kt),
d = distance in miles.

---

[12] Project *Cantaloupe*: USAF study of nuclear explosions in space for anti-missile defence (*Republic Aviation News*, December 9, 1960).

In principle, it is not possible to detonate a nuclear warhead unless the fissionable materials form a critical mass, but if the components are large enough to amplify each fission occurring, an incoming neutron will set off many other fissions within the ICBM. This amplification could lead to an internal release of energy, producing temperature changes and inhibit the operation of the warhead.[13]

Electronic systems proper can also be affected by nuclear radiation, and present-day designs are vulnerable to a 1-Mt explosion in vacuum at a distance of 100 miles (10^7 r/sec). With improved circuits—e.g. General Electric's *Thermionic Integrated Micro-Modules* (TIMM)—constructed only of metals and ceramics, the lethal distance would be reduced to thirteen miles (10^9 r/sec).[14]

A point to be remembered is that nuclear deflagrations in space may seriously disrupt radio communications and the radar warning network. This was suggested as a result of certain US tests (Project *Argus*) in August and September 1958, when three Lockheed *X-17* solid-propellant rockets were fired, each carrying a 1 to $1\frac{1}{2}$-kt warhead.

ANCILLARY, SUPPORTING AND LOGISTIC SYSTEMS

The third major class of orbital vehicles and devices comprises reconnaissance, early warning, surveillance, identification, navigation, communication and meteorology satellites. Some of these devices are shown in Fig. 9.

Broadly, these orbiters can be classified as follows:

1. *Reconnaissance, early warning and surveillance:* ground inspection of foreign territories—photographic (TV or recoverable film cameras), infra-red and radar systems. This would include search for suspected rocket-launching sites and early warning of launches by infra-red sensors.

2. *Satellite identification:* orbitals designed to locate, interrogate, photograph and identify unscheduled vehicles in orbital space. In the early stages of development this could be performed

---

[13] *Missiles and Rockets,* January 30, 1961.
[14] *Scientific American,* April 1961, p. 133.

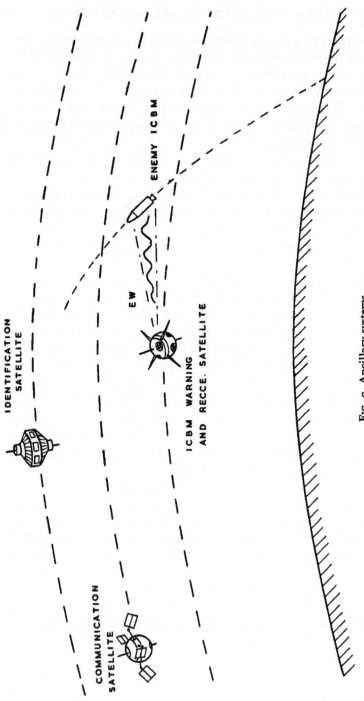

FIG. 9. Ancillary systems.

by a special form of defence missile, launched to meet the unknown object in its orbit. In certain respects guidance techniques will be similar to those of anti-orbital weapons. As an example of overlapping duties, the location, interrogation and identification can also be performed by anti-satellite orbiters such as the recent Westinghouse project already mentioned.

3. *Navigation and mapping:* accurate positional fixes of enemy IRBMS, FBMS and ICBMS—both fixed and mobile.

4. *Communications:* rapid transmission of surveillance, reconnaissance and other information to home stations.

5. *Meteorology:* routine inspection of global weather conditions. This type of orbital can perform other duties, such as surveillance.

A US authority had stated that early-warning satellites could double the warning time now expected through the long-range radar network. It was also suggested that orbitals equipped to detect ballistic-missile launches will supplement or even replace ground-based systems and should thus become one of the keystones of the North American defence system.

Modified forms of early-warning orbiters could also be used for peacetime nuclear-test control and surveillance, provided an agreement is reached between the nations concerned.

The launches of the detector satellite *Midas 3* and of the weather satellite *Tiros 3* have already had some political repercussions. Towards the end of July 1961 an article appeared in the Soviet military journal *Red Star* denouncing the USA for orbiting these two devices over Russian territory. It argued that "a spy is still a spy at whatever height it flies" and described the launchings as "acts of aggression". No further action was taken by USSR at the time of writing, but the protest is indicative of Soviet reactions to reconnaissance and weather orbiters circulating over their territory. Thus, it is logical to expect that in due course the Russians will attempt to interfere with these satellites, possibly by direct interception.

Mapping and charting are very important; it is known that the present-day world coverage contains a number of errors, in some cases sufficient to impair the accuracy of surface-to-surface

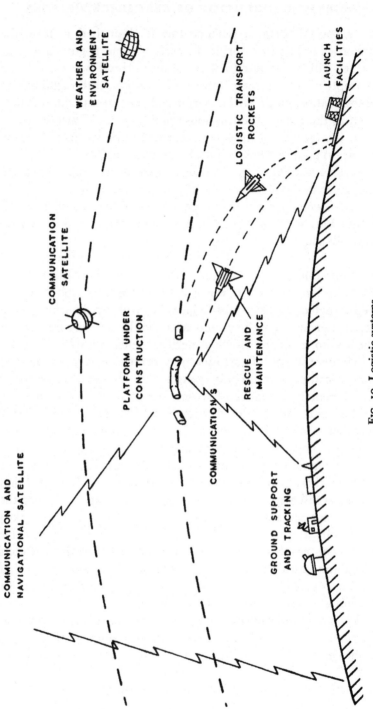

TO HIGH ORBIT
COMMUNICATION AND
NAVIGATIONAL SATELLITE

COMMUNICATION
SATELLITE

WEATHER AND
ENVIRONMENT
SATELLITE

PLATFORM UNDER
CONSTRUCTION

LOGISTIC TRANSPORT
ROCKETS

COMMUNICATIONS

RESCUE AND
MAINTENANCE

GROUND SUPPORT
AND TRACKING

LAUNCH
FACILITIES

FIG. 10. Logistic systems.

ballistic or space-to-surface missiles. In this connection the USAF are considering the development of an orbiter providing a very high resolution pictorial image. The satellite would carry a 40-ft focal length camera capable of distinguishing 1-ft-long objects from an altitude of from 300 to 350 miles.[15]

Further development of orbital vehicles and devices will lead to the appearance of systems corresponding to the supply services of surface forces and the key term to this family of vehicles is *logistic*. Variable orbit capability will be mandatory; large payload requirements will give rise to a demand for boosters with very high thrust ratings. A typical supporting system is represented in Fig. 10.

Projects SLOMAR, SMART and *Phoenix* mentioned earlier in this chapter belong to the logistic class of orbitals.

MANNED FLIGHT AND FURTHER DEVELOPMENTS

The first phase of orbital armament development will consist of unmanned devices such as observation satellites, communication orbiters and early forms of defensive weapons, e.g. anti-orbitals. The development of human space flight will be pursued in parallel, but at this stage it might be premature to construct a full-scale military aerospace doctrine on the assumption of manned operations before 1970. In other words, the various weapons and devices belonging to the first era will be of the "robot" variety, programmed or tele-controlled from the ground.

As mentioned earlier, the first US *manned military aerospace vehicle* will be a boost-glider of the Boeing *DynaSoar* type (Plate 5, facing p. 98). The time it is likely to spend outside the atmosphere will be comparatively short, hence it is unlikely that radiation and other environmental hazards would have a major effect upon the crew and reduce its operational efficiency.

The advent of manned "environment proof" satellite platforms will accelerate progress and eventually the centre of gravity of global strategic operations may shift into orbital space. If this hypothesis is correct, Powers contending for space

[15] *Aviation Week*, December 12, 1960.

supremacy will have to extend their influence farther out into space. For example, indications abound in the technical Press concerning Moon projects, from . hard-landing probes to manned ships—e.g. Project *Nova* (Plate 10, facing p. 114).

An example of even more advanced thinking is the Convair Feasibility Study *Orion* (Plate 11, facing p. 115). The vehicles envisaged, ranging from 1,000 to 65,000 tons at lift-off, would be driven by water or ablating propellant and nuclear charges exploding in sequence, the new concept of power plant being described as *capsulated nuclear-charge propulsion*. This particular study illustrates the scope and boldness of new concepts being evaluated in connection with astronautics proper, i.e. travel in outer space.

*

For some time now US military planners have been freely discussing the possibility of using the Moon as an early-warning station and, eventually, as a *bombardment site*. Evidently account must be taken of environmental problems to be solved, but it may be of interest to summarize here the general trend of thought in USA.

Published information suggests that a number of studies were made by major firms under the sponsorship of US Government agencies. For instance, according to Brigadier-General Homer A. Boushey:

". . . if the US had a base on the Moon, any enemy, the Soviet Union or any other Power, would have to launch an overwhelming nuclear attack toward the Moon from its own land bases two-and-a-half days before attacking the continental USA, or face certain and massive destruction from Moon bases forty-eight hours after it attacked the USA."[16]

Over two years ago a Westinghouse study of a lunar base was mentioned in the Press, analysing the advantages and disadvantages of launching, say, a 1-Mt nuclear warhead from the Moon. As pointed out by General Boushey, it would have

[16] *Aviation Week*, April 28, 1958.

the distinct advantage of a deterrent weapon not easily neutral-ized by surprise attack, but the economics of building and supplying a lunar launching site appeared to be unsound, bearing in mind that an ICBM could fulfil a similar mission at a lift-off weight of, say, 100,000 to 300,000 lb, as against a lunar vehicle of some 4 million lb.

Presentations were made by various constructors under ARDC, USAF, System Requirement SR-183,[17] which envisaged the establishment of a lunar observatory. Basic characteristics of the requirement were similar in many respects to the more advanced formulation, designated SR-192, relating to retalia-tory bombardment capability from a Moon base. Additionally, a broad USAF study was mentioned (SR-182) summarizing the requirements of vehicles and weapons operating beyond the Moon, in interplanetary space.

The efficiency of a surveillance base on the Moon was queried. For instance, the percentage of time the Earth could present reasonable viewing per day and per year is limited. Studies under SR-183, which were in effect feasibility evaluations, con-sidered all methods of surveillance—optics, infra-red, radar and other procedures. Optics were not favoured on account of cloud obliteration.

The proposals discussed at the briefing included the follow-ing:

(a) Vehicle for lunar mission accommodating up to ten men.

(b) For the voyage out, probably four stages of propulsion would be required and two stages for the return from the Moon, making a total of six.

(c) One booster scheme envisaged a cluster of liquid pro-pellant rocket motors developing a total thrust of 16 million lb. Another plan assumed the use of a large cluster of solid pro-pellant rockets for booster service. Nuclear propulsion in the form of a single stage for the outward journey was also proposed, but for an operational date in the 1970s.

(d) Estimates of lift-off weights of the lunar vehicle varied from about 5 million lb up.

[17] Superseded by Study Requirement 17532.

It must be remembered, however, that all these discussions date back to 1958 and that, since then, considerable progress has been made in astronautical technology. Earlier, in Chapter III, the US Moon programme was mentioned and also the alleged Russian time-table. Thus, projects which sounded somewhat far-fetched three years ago now begin to look more reasonable, nearer to what could be described as the *possibility stage*.

The current very high costs of "space transportation" are primarily due to research and development still needed for a rapid transition from vehicles of uneconomical size, from "one-shot" launchers and inefficient application of chemical propulsion. The costs do not result from any inherently high energy requirements in space flight. This, in fact, is a fundamental misconception.

Take the following three categories of Earth-Moon travel cost assessment:

1. Extremely conservative estimates.

2. Estimates allowing for a probable reduction of costs.

3. Ultimately possible, even without new theoretical knowledge.

Adopting the 1965 values for these three categories, the following figures were assumed:

Category 1: $100,000 per lb of payload.

Category 2: $5,000 per lb of payload.

Category 3: $1,000 per lb of payload.

Further estimates show that every five years the cost per lb of payload should decrease by one order of magnitude. For instance, in 1970 the corresponding figures would be $10,000, $500 and $100 respectively. Extrapolating to 1980, and taking Category 2 as an example, the cost per lb of payload could be reduced to $5.[18]

As indicated in Chapter IV, the actual costs of existing space vehicles are difficult to determine from published information, but the following empirical expression was derived from *Juno 2*, *Thor Delta*, *Thor Agena B*, *Atlas Centaur* and *Saturn C-1* estimates:

[18] *Astronautics*, June 1961.

$$C_s = \frac{620,000}{W_p^{0.7}},$$

where: C_s = cost in $ per lb of payload in orbit (launch
                costs excluded),
        W_p = payload in pounds.

However theoretical, these figures seem to indicate that the rapid development of astronautical technology may well lead to a drastic reduction of costs, even in the case of interplanetary journeys.

CHAPTER VI

Aerospace in World Politics and Strategy

The trends reviewed in the previous chapter clearly indicate the importance of new aerospace techniques in the realm of world strategy. A gradual evolution of present-day and near-future ballistic missiles into a more sophisticated system is to be expected: the connecting links between the strategic bomber and strategic missile on the one hand and future aerospace armaments, on the other, will be the *recallable* ICBM and glide-boost bomber of the Boeing *DynaSoar* class. Evidently there is no valid reason for this development to stop at some comparatively simple form of aerospace vehicle or device.

From the moment manned military satellites become feasible, the vehicles discussed in Chapter V will appear in the construction programmes of the "Big U" Powers. It is difficult to estimate the time scale, but the accelerating rate of development from *Sputnik 1* (1957) to the *Vostok* satellites (1961) suggests that seemingly optimistic forecasts may not be wholly unjustified.

Further advances in strategic thinking are now likely to occur, prompted by the Russian *Man-in-Orbit* successes. Since even conventional military thought is finally influenced by new technological developments, some aspects of the present-day deterrent doctrine will be re-evaluated and modernized.

*

The most important novel feature of aerospace armaments is that an orbital conflict is conceivable, without necessarily triggering off a major nuclear conflagration on the surface of the globe. The study of this idea will be the main theme of the present chapter, and as an opening gambit it could be said that the surface-based ballistic missile *Deterrent-in-Being* will gradually be devalued. The new orbital action concept may then take the form of a *Deterrent-in-Action*.

In a recent book [1] Herman Kahn of RAND Corporation questioned the assumption that nuclear war is "unthinkable". He put forward various suggestions as to the best way of reducing the number of casualties; in other words, treating an atomic conflict as a more or less predictable form of warfare.

It is true that there is evidence of USSR developing a comprehensive programme of protection of the population. This defence effort is on a compulsory basis: units, down to collective farms and blocks of flats, are called upon to organize self-defence groups made up of fire-fighters, shelter-marshals and medical personnel. Massive Civil Defence training began in 1955 and it is claimed that 10 per cent. of the population have been enlisted. It is also significant, however, that a new trend in Soviet Civil Defence is to evacuate the inhabitants of target cities to initial staging areas ten to fifty miles outside the urban limits. In 1961 compulsory courses will give the CD formations in all major towns sixty-four hours training in evacuation procedures. [2]

No doubt the first effects of a nuclear attack can be alleviated by an efficient Civil Defence system, but new methods of employment of fusion weapons, e.g. multi-megaton high bursts, could create an entirely new situation where resulting fire storms, starvation and disease might well claim as many victims as an equivalent number of megatons acting directly at low level.

The present author does not wish to embark upon a contro-

[1] *On Thermonuclear War*, by Herman Kahn, Princeton University, 1960. An interesting critique of this book appeared in *Scientific American*, March 1961.
[2] *Time*, February 10, 1961.

versy, but merely refers to the revival of conventional defence concepts in an attempt to evade the evident deadlock in conventional nuclear armaments.

A much more interesting concept is the so-called *Panama Hypothesis*. The object and contents of this theory are summarized in the following abstract from an American technical journal[3]:

"To date, only one reason for urgency in our space programme has been adequately presented and has achieved any general acceptance; that is the issue of national prestige. While this reason alone is cause for concern, there are other reasons which may have even greater impact on our national future. One such reason—the *Panama Hypothesis*—will be discussed here.

"The Panama Hypothesis can be summarized in this statement: there are strategic areas of space—vital to future scientific, military, and commercial space programmes—which must be occupied by the United States, lest their use be ever denied us through prior occupation by unfriendly powers.

". . . The Panama Theory rests on at least five conditions and possibly some others which have not been identified. Although none of the five can be proved at this time, all are highly probable and all rest squarely on strong historical precedents. The five conditions are as follows:

1. *Life in space:* the ability of man to live and work beyond the Earth's atmosphere.

2. *Low transportation costs:* the ability of our technology to reduce space transportation costs to reasonably low levels eventually.

3. *The need:* the scientific, military, economic, and sociopolitical reasons for extra-terrestrial colonies;

4. *Preferred or strategic areas:* the critical importance of the Moon itself and the almost certain existence of relatively few key areas on the Moon.

5. *International competition:* even under a condition of general world disarmament, economic competition would continue, particularly between Communist countries and the Free World.

[3] *Astronautics,* June 1961.

Russia might claim lunar Panamas, if in a position to do so, and thus acquire significant advantage in the future exploration and development of the solar system. . . ."

The *Panama Hypothesis* may sound an exaggeration of future possibilities, but in the author's view it is also a very healthy sign of imaginative thinking in an area of knowledge almost totally neglected in Western Europe.

*

For the purpose of the present study it will be supposed that an orbital war can assume two related forms. The conflict may be limited either to *cold war* resulting in "accidents" in space, or—after a period of comparatively peaceful technical competition—break out into a *hot* or *shooting war* in orbit. The salutary fear of wholesale destruction on the surface of the Earth should prevent orbital incidents degenerating into World War III.

The general trend of argument developed in this chapter is not really affected by the actual sequence of events: the hypothetical evolution of aerospace strategy can be subdivided into two arbitrary sections merely as a convenient method of presenting two alternatives or forms of the same phenomenon.

The overall pattern of events to be examined is that of *attrition*. This term indicates that the process under consideration is not simply a technical race, but an intermittent series of clashes between vehicles and devices in space.

For instance, collisions in space may follow some acrimonious exchanges between the Governments concerned as to the rights or wrongs of reconnaissance and observation from orbit. It will be remembered that the launching of US *Tiros* produced an adverse reaction in the Soviet Press, but the Kremlin did not press the argument any further and the matter was dropped. It is thought, however, that the incident was symptomatic and the chances are that similar outbreaks, but in a much more acute form will occur in the near future.

Protests, stormy scenes at UN and fruitless controversies

about sovereign rights in space will add fuel to the fire and eventually the day will dawn when an orbiter belonging to nation *A* will be destroyed by an anti-orbital device launched by nation *B*. Again, this is unlikely to lead to anything much except a renewal of violent protests and more mutual abuse; nevertheless it will be an historical military event—*the first combat in orbital space*.

The scientific and technological struggle between USA and USSR will become more intense and both sides will be compelled to devote more and more resources to aerospace work in order to maintain some measure of parity. The number of incidents in orbit would also increase and every effort will be made to counteract the effects of hostile interventions in space. This will take the form of both technological improvement of vehicles and devices and of an increasing number of launches with the object of compensating for losses sustained in the course of the *process of attrition*.

It is also likely that there will be periods of armistice, appeals to disarmament and various other political moves to gain time to build up a more powerful space armoury. Since orbital incidents are unlikely to degenerate into a World War, the stimulus present in the case of Surface Disarmament Conferences will be missing. In other words, almost by tacit agreement, both major opponents will strive to achieve superiority in space, realizing that any major repercussions on the surface might be equally dangerous to both parties. It follows that there is little likelihood of orbital disarmament; "Space Law" will probably continue to be a suitable subject for learned debates, but without any practical results. The struggle for supremacy in aerospace will at least demonstrate the fallacy of such notions as "Laws of War".

*

If the hypothesis outlined above is borne out by future events, the process of *attrition in space* will exert considerable influence

PLATE 9
Project
Saturn
(left)

PLATE 10
Project
Nova
(right)

Scale of Feet

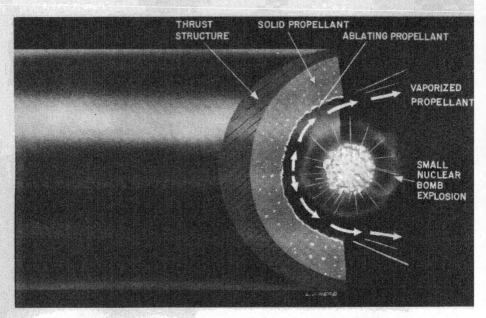

THRUST
STRUCTURE

SOLID PROPELLANT

ABLATING PROPELLANT

VAPORIZED
PROPELLANT

SMALL
NUCLEAR
BOMB
EXPLOSION

PLATE 11. The propulsion system of Project *Orion*.

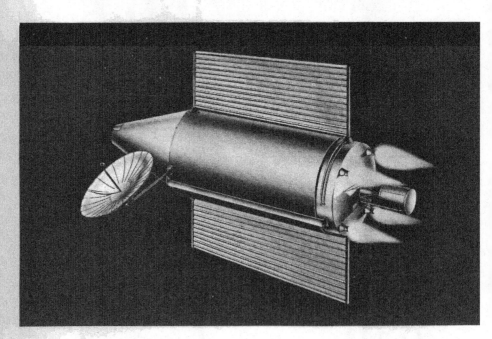

PLATE 12. Avco project of thermal arc (electric) rockets as a low-thrust, long-endurance cruising power plant. Hydrogen propellant, electric power supplied from nuclear source.

[facing p. 115]

upon the global political and strategic situation. Very gradually the world status of nations unarmed in orbit and space will deteriorate and their influence in world affairs diminish accordingly. In the somewhat artificial atmosphere of UN the various "uncommitted" Afro-Asian states will no doubt want to contribute their views, but in terms of Grand Strategy and military balance of power opinions thus expressed can only be of academic interest. Thus *aerospace power* might become an attribute of nations with a real say in world matters.

An orbital conflict between two major Powers, without the possibility of any other nation influencing its outcome, will demonstrate the unfortunate but evident futility of "words without weapons" and create a growing sense of insecurity among the population of the globe. The effect would be purely psychological, but as a corollary, acute partisanship is likely to develop, fluctuating with the fortunes of the space war. In other words, the presently profitable neutralism will tend to become a risky policy, since the winner of the space struggle might well achieve a more or less unpleasant form of world supremacy. In a political climate of this nature counting votes at UN or some such assembly becomes a meaningless occupation.

Orbital war may effectively supersede peripheral conflicts and other forms of Cold War. While Korean-type incidents and political crises at UN are unlikely to produce decisive results, sustained orbital attrition involving the destruction of circulating vehicles and devices should eventually result in the technical and strategic preponderance of one of the contestants.

Reverting to the probable sequence of events, the initial technological race is already in progress, combined with the USA-USSR competition in ballistic missile armaments. Unless a major war intervenes, it is to be expected that the Americans will succeed in closing the "Missile Gap" and by the end of 1964 a position of parity will be restored, possibly followed by a phase of Western superiority. In the meantime the development of aerospace vehicles and devices, as distinct from ballistic missiles, will proceed at an increasing pace. As suggested, *hostilities* might begin in the form of "incidents" in orbit; the ensuing process of attrition would be a lengthy one, the opponents bringing into action series of improved or new types of orbiters and supporting sub-systems.

Space will become populated by a number of vehicles and devices, armed or unarmed, circulating in various orbits. If by then manned space flight reaches operational status, the control and monitoring of weapons and devices will be gradually taken over by special space platforms. Since these stations can be of the offensive and defensive type and unless some clear zones of action are defined and agreed upon by the two contenders, clashes resulting in loss of human life will be inevitable.

If technical and military parity is maintained in orbital space up to a state where fleets of vehicles are in constant operation, the opponents may be tempted to resolve the static crisis by a full-scale aerospace war. Also, war in orbit may not necessarily be the result of a conscious decision taken by one of the opponents, but simply due to the tension created by the presence of potentially-hostile vehicles in the same regions of orbital space.

Once an open conflict begins, it is unlikely that discussions at UN, Summit Meetings and other rhetorical exercises would succeed in stopping it. The writer would like to emphasize here that even a deliberate *shooting* conflict in space need not trigger off any major military reactions on the surface. The lethal potential of surface armaments will still exist and it can be expected that the orbital conflict will be localized, by mutual tacit consent. This does not mean, however, that the psychological impact on public opinion will not be great: it is more than likely that a Government unable to distract public attention from the premonitory signs of losing the battle will find itself in a very serious predicament.

Even in a country closely supervised by a powerful police system, it will be difficult, if not altogether impossible to conceal from the population the eventual annihilation of the nation's space force. Morale must necessarily suffer and the remedy might be the creation of a *kamikaze* state of mind on a nation-wide basis. This is an improbable solution and it is suggested that finally the loser of the orbital war will have to accept the dictates of the victor. This need not take the primitive form of an ultimatum of unconditional surrender, driving the vanquished to desperate action, but simply lead to a change of political régime which will permit the gradual adjustment of policies to those of the Power in command of aerospace.

A simpler alternative might be that instead of aerospace parity being maintained, one side will achieve complete technical supremacy. This would result in an increasing loss of power equilibrium between the two opponents and finally a point may be reached where it will become obvious even to the uninformed observer that one of the competitors had irretrievably lost the latent aerospace war.

At this stage it might be worth reminding the reader of the problem of retaliation by surface weapons raised in Chapter V. Let us consider a situation where two equally well-armed nations—A and B—become involved in an orbital conflict or state of attrition. It must be remembered that our hypothesis assumes that neither side wishes to start a major nuclear war on the surface; if it were not so, the probability is that World War III would take place before orbital weapons become operational.

The first phase of the conflict would be localized in orbit. Now suppose that A, after a prolonged struggle, destroys B's space force. This leaves the victor in a position of mastery in orbital space, though B may still be capable of launching antiorbitals to interfere with A's aerospace fleet.

B will now be faced with the dilemma of either letting A grow stronger and stronger in aerospace, or of starting a preventive war on the surface. This, in itself, is contrary to the principle of *dissuasion* and even under the most favourable conditions will invite a retaliatory attack by A since it is improbable that the damage inflicted by B upon A would totally eliminate the latter's surface weapons.

As a result B will be exposed to both the reaction of A's remaining surface weapons and to a major if not crushing counterattack from orbit. Incidentally, there is nothing B can do to ensure adequate warning or devise a system of defence against A's aerospace retaliation.

The above reasoning does not take into account the fact that since A is in full control of orbital space, the concealment of surface weapons, particularly of rocket launches, becomes a difficult proposition. What is more, no account is taken of the possible intervention of aerospace anti-ICBM and anti-IRBM devices. In the present state of the art it seems that surface-launched anti-ballistic missiles will not be very effective. On the other hand, weapons circulating in space—combined with satellite warning and reconnaissance systems—are more likely to be able to intercept and destroy high-trajectory missiles.

Therefore it does seem that B—without any orbital cover —will be in a very vulnerable position: the final choice will lie between a *kamikaze* apotheosis on a national scale or a "conditional surrender" in the form of a realignment with the policies and social structure of A.

*

It is an interesting thought that an orbital conflict of the type described would be oddly reminiscent of feudal wars in the Middle Ages. The mass of the population, allies and even "uncommitted" nations, will be the burghers and villeins, helpless spectators of the clash of machines in space, without any possibility of influencing the final outcome. Thus, in accordance with the medieval archetype, the fate of large communities may be decided by a comparatively small group of people. One of the main differences will be that instead of simple and cheap transport and armament consisting of horses, swords, lances and armour, aerospace forces will demand gigantic budgets and massive support by a vast number of "technical serfs".

Finally, a curious paradox may arise; namely, that the emergence of very advanced weapon systems such as orbitals, combined with new agents of destruction, could well inhibit a virtually suicidal and therefore pointless war on the surface of the globe. The winner of the space war would then be in a position to dictate terms not only to the losing side but to all its allies and "uncommitted" nations. In fact, a World Government would be created, but bearing little resemblance to the Utopian dreams of those who seem to be constitutionally unable to comprehend the grim realities of twentieth-century Power Politics.

*

To complete the present chapter it is proposed to review the role which could be played by USA's allies, China and the "uncommitted" nations. Starting with UK and the Commonwealth—in combination with Western Europe—it is unlikely that this "Third" or rather "Fourth Force" could intervene decisively in an aerospace war. It is not only a question of budgets and manpower: Euromarket statistics show that the combined economic and industrial potential of Western Europe is comparable to that of USA. The reasons are firstly political and military disunity and, secondly, the lack of understanding of future Grand Strategy.[4] As a result the technological gap with respect to USA and USSR in aerospace matters has become such that it can no longer be closed.

It can only be hoped that strategic requirements will be reassessed in the near future and steps taken to remedy the situation as far as possible. Western European members of NATO should consider complementing their existing forces, best suited for localized European incidents, by some form of reconnaissance and anti-satellite armament to take over the surveillance and defence of certain limited zones of orbital space.

A programme of this nature is not very ambitious for a united Western Europe with a population of some 200 million.

[4] With a few noteworthy exceptions, e.g. General L.-M. Chassin's article "Vue sur la Guerre Spatiale", in *Forces Aériennes Françaises*, No. 163, October 1960.

Apart from military and scientific uses, this is likely to pay indirect dividends; for instance, in the form of applications of new discoveries and techniques in industries unrelated to aerospace.

Western European nations must build up a strong cadre of scientists and technicians fully conversant with the latest developments in astronautics. If such a cadre were established, Western Europe could give appreciable help to USA. American programmes will be loaded with an increasing inventory of increasingly expensive hardware; eventually, the major portion of the defence effort may be absorbed by the build-up, maintenance, operation and support of an aerospace force on a global scale. The very considerable research and development requirements of such a force will demand additional *brain power*; USA having a vast number of other commitments—in addition to the maintenance of a normal industrial life and of a high standard of living—Western Europe should be in a position to help by taking over certain lines of advanced research.

Initial laboratory research in the field of electric propulsion need not be very costly, and well within the competence of European scientists. Also, depending upon the magnitude of programmes envisaged, Western European aerospace industries could undertake work more akin to advanced aeronautics; for instance, the design and development of winged vehicles of the ferry-ship type.

*

Once more Red China appears as an unknown quantity, but while Mao Tse Tung's régime may eventually produce some form of nuclear weapon, it is highly unlikely that within the next twenty years the former Celestial Empire could undertake an aerospace programme on a scale comparable with USA and USSR.

Politically speaking, the Soviets will have considerable difficulties with their south-eastern neighbours, but fortunately for

Russia the geography and population pattern of China are such as to make her very vulnerable to multi-megaton, heavy fall-out and biological weapons. Thus, as far as the present study is concerned, Chinese intervention in a space conflict between USA and USSR is improbable.

The political influence of various "uncommitted" nations is mainly dependent upon an ambient atmosphere of Cold War: the nationalistic and anti-West outbursts of Africans and Asians will sound impressive only so long as the two major nuclear-armed opponents hold each other in check. It is not difficult to imagine what would happen if a certain Power were to achieve supremacy—particularly against a background of appeals by Mr. Nehru and speeches by Dr. Nkrumah. The final answer to undesirable incidents would lie in aerospace: under the cover of global weapons, *Sky Cavalry* formations should have no difficulty in restoring order. In an emergency, a local demonstration of nuclear or biological warfare would soon bring to reason any dissenting community or state still under the spell of past glories of UN meetings and debates.

CHAPTER VII

Scientific and Civil Applications of Astronautics

Strictly speaking, a detailed review of scientific and civil applications of aerospace techniques is outside the scope of the present book. It must be remembered, however, that non-military programmes are closely related to developments in the aerospace weapon field: whatever pious intentions scientists may express as to the ultimate aims of their space research work, the fact remains that, one way or another, the main bulk of disposable funds is invariably provided from defence budgets.

A number of physicists and astronomers have now become interested in astronautics, but on the whole, in countries where aerospace work is in its infancy, there is still a distinct lack of attention to the more advanced engineering aspects of the problem. Priority is given to physical and astronomical research, the instrument-carrying vehicles being taken more or less for granted—in some cases simply to be "hired" from USA.

Reversing the argument, it could be said that astronautics—as the science and technology of *locomotion* outside the terrestrial atmosphere—is not uniquely concerned with the scientific experiments or observations performed by the payloads of space vehicles. Broadly speaking, the astronomer or physicist is the *passenger* and the astronautical engineer is the *carrier*. In Western Europe there seems to be some confusion with regard to aerospace work and little progress will be made in this field until the distinction between Government agencies and Industry is clearly understood and zones of activity defined.

This does not mean that environmental research is of no

interest to the aerospace engineer: the vehicles and devices mentioned in the present chapter will make important contributions to the general pool of astronautical technology. Nevertheless, in the context of the present essay, scientific research is valuable inasmuch as it will enable aerospace designers and constructors to achieve a higher degree of technical and operational efficiency.

*

In the absence of a better term, non-scientific and non-military applications of aerospace vehicles and devices will be described as *civil*, i.e. devices that can be exploited on a commercial basis by concerns operating for the express purpose of earning dividends for their shareholders.

At first civil applications of early forms of aerospace vehicles seemed improbable, but a closer study of the subject revealed that communications satellites can fulfil a political and commercial role, as distinct from military applications. For instance, the administrative and economic cohesion of geographically-dispersed units such as the British Commonwealth and the Communauté Française is partly dependent upon the existence of an independent and efficient communication network; the indications are that orbiters may provide improved facilities.

In the interests of brevity, the discussion will be limited to a number of typical vehicles and devices. Table 23 (Appendix I, p. 138) gives a summary of satellites and probes launched by the Americans and the Russians up to July 1, 1961.[1]

Table 21 overleaf gives a summary of successful launchings over the same period. It is interesting that 76 per cent. were American orbiters.

In recent years a vast number of drawings and photographs of various space devices have been published in the Press. Plates 6 and 7 are included in the text to illustrate two important types of US and USSR orbiters.

The area of research which is very important from the

[1] *Aviation Week and Space Technology*, August 7, 1961.

TABLE 21   *Summary of successful launchings*
up to July 1, 1961 (Satellites and probes)

Year	Number of launchings						Total launchings
	USA		USSR		Total		
	In orbit	Decayed	In orbit	Decayed	In orbit	Decayed	
1957 & 1958	2	5	—	3	2	8	10
1959	5	6	1	2	6	8	14
1960	9	7	1	2	10	9	19
1st half 1961	9	1	1	4	10	5	15
Totals	25	19	3	11	28	30	58

Note: Satellite and capsule or multiple orbitals counted as a single launching.

military point of view comprises space biology and psychology, the general study of environment—particularly of radiation—and the evaluation of hazards such as collisions with meteorites. No doubt a great deal of useful information has already been collected, but it remains to be seen whether the Powers performing these observations and experiments will disclose the full results. From the security point of view it might be considered preferable to withhold certain vital data, not to give a potential enemy a valuable lead, particularly with regard to the possibilities of manned space flight on an operational scale.

Starting with *Sounding Rockets*, it can be said these are the simplest form of aerospace device, mainly used for the exploration of the upper atmosphere. Equipped with a number of miniature instruments, sounding rockets can furnish valuable information about the structure of the upper strata of the air space surrounding the Earth. Thus, variations of temperature and pressure with altitude, intensity and distribution of radiation and data about the velocity, rate of impact and mass of cosmic particles in the vicinity of the Earth were obtained in USA in 1946 with the former *V-2*, in 1949 with the *Viking*, and in the early 1950s with *Aerobee* rockets.

The payloads of these devices were of the order of 150 lb, and the altitudes reached did not exceed 700 miles. Current programmes provide for more advanced types of vehicles carrying less payload, but extending their field of research well beyond 1,000 miles. Originally a great disadvantage of this form of investigation was the ultimate destruction of instruments, but the latest models are equipped with recoverable nose cones.

Sounding rockets are much cheaper than orbitals, but they all have one common drawback—their very short duration of measurement. Thus, a logical step forward was the scientific application of satellites.

Orbitals can be put to a number of uses, and pictorial recording may be quoted as the first example. Observation can be made by using sensors operating in different portions of the electromagnetic spectrum, extending from the purely visual, by photography, to the most modern radar and infra-red systems.

Photogrammetry is a highly developed branch of surveying, but up to the present only a fraction of the Earth's surface has been adequately mapped to required modern standards. Orbitals will assist and speed up the conventional procedure, the chief advantage of the satellite being its high altitude. Photographic films exposed aboard an orbiter are stored until the satellite is in the vicinity of the ground receiving station; the picture is then transmitted, using a television technique, or the film is returned to Earth in a capsule.

Astronomical photography by satellites has the advantage of eliminating the obscuring effect of the atmosphere.

As mentioned earlier, radiation and environmental investigations probably head the list of scientific uses of satellites. It will be sufficient to mention here geodetic observations and the measurements of the total magnetic field, solar radiation, X-rays and gamma rays, electron density, streams of solar protons and other elementary particles, densities of solar corona, micro-meteorites and ionosphere. The experiments on growth of spores and yeast in space, plant growth cycle under conditions of weightlessness and tests of the effects of space environment on mammals is another area for scientific investigation.

Improved observational quality and larger volume of data would require a greater power supply; if a man is to control operations, the total payload carried will rise sharply. This is inevitable if knowledge of outer space is to improve beyond the limits imposed by the restricted capabilities of automatic or tele-controlled devices.

Manned observation orbitals could carry telescopes to obtain spectra of planets, stars and galaxies—from ultra-violet to infrared and atomic clocks will be used to test the General Theory of relativity.

Satellite cloud observation will add continuity and generally complement the present Earth-bound meteorological system. Surprisingly good results have already been obtained from an accurate cloud analysis, particularly in areas where no other means of weather forecasting are available.

In addition to cloud observation, the weather satellite can be equipped with a variety of infra-red sensors which would scan the surface of the Earth. It is claimed that these infra-red observations give temperatures at various altitudes and the heat balance of the area under observation. Since "weather" is nothing else but a visible manifestation of the reactions of the atmosphere to the amount of heat or energy absorbed by the various gases and the underlying surface, information on the heat balance is a necessary prerequisite to accurate long-range forecasting.

Many cosmic probes or artificial planets will have to be launched in order to determine the characteristics of deep space environment. Measurements similar to those conducted in the vicinity of the Earth and of the Moon must be made around Mars and Venus before man can be expected to land on their surface.

Much more information is needed about the sporadic outbursts of solar radiation. These outbursts, also known as *flares*, might well be the most formidable obstacle to space travel. Only a complete knowledge of their intensity, frequency and magnitude would enable man to find ways of defending himself against their deadly radiation effects. It may be of interest to mention here a US proposal to establish around the vehicle an artificial electromagnetic field which would deflect the "rays": the idea appears attractive, but the very large power requirements makes it impracticable in the present state of technology.

Most important from the point of view of both celestial mechanics and of the theory of relativity are the measurements of gravitational fields in space. Here cosmic probes will find extensive applications.

*

A definition of civil space vehicles was given earlier in the present chapter, but the real test is whether a given design can be exploited commercially by a private or State-subsidized concern; in fact, Government help will be required in all cases where the applications are primarily of national interest. A good example is the communications orbital.

Basically there are two classes of communications satellites —*active* and *passive*. The former carries transmitting equipment designed to receive a signal from the ground, amplify it and relay it back to Earth—either immediately or after a set delay, via suitable recorders, in pictorial or audible form.

The passive communication satellite merely reflects or scatters incident radiation from the Earth.[2]

One of the first types of communication orbiters considered was the twenty-four-hour or *stationary* device.[3] If its orbit is circular and at a height of 22,300 miles from the surface of the Earth, the period of rotation is twenty-four hours. Assuming that the satellite moves in the equatorial plane and in the same direction as the Earth's rotation, it will remain stationary over some point over the Equator. It will keep in view the same area (just less than one-half) of the Earth's surface and three

[2] e.g. US *Echo* in a 1,000-mile orbit.
[3] The US programme includes the 1,000 lb *Advent* communication satellite which is to be launched into a 22,300-mile orbit in 1963.

stationary orbitals would thus provide constant global coverage, except for the polar regions.

While theoretically the stationary satellite scheme appears to be very effective, it has certain characteristics which, at this stage of development, make it somewhat difficult to implement.

Firstly, the establishment of a 22,300-mile orbit would require a fairly large vehicle, if a commercially-adequate payload is to be put in circulation at that altitude. Secondly, it is mandatory to synchronize all orbiters with great precision since relative "creep" between the three units would eventually disrupt the network of communications. The launch and guidance accuracy required would be of a very high order and in practice periodical corrections may have to be applied by low-thrust long-endurance propulsion units. This means that some form of auxiliary rocket motor will have to be developed, possibly of the plasma type.

It is more likely, therefore, that the early generations of communication satellites will orbit at much lower altitudes—somewhere around 300 miles—in elliptical paths. Their life will be limited by residual air drag, but there is a school of thought advocating that a properly launched commercial orbiter should survive long enough to pay its depreciation costs and earn considerable profit.[5]

As an illustration of possible commercial applications the proposed time-tables of three companies are given below:[6]

1. *American Telephone and Telegraph Company:* low altitude polar orbit, could be in operation within three or four years; the first of several experimental satellites could be delivered by December 1961, if permission to use launching facilities were promptly obtained.

2. *General Electric:* first five of a ten-satellite, 6,000-mile orbit equatorial system could be operational by mid-1964, with a complete system by mid-1965.

3. *Lockheed:* two synchronous satellites orbiting at 22,300

[5] The recovery of boosters (*flyback systems*) would greatly reduce the operational costs of satellites.

[6] *Aviation Week*, May 8, 1961.

miles in equatorial orbit over the Atlantic and two over the Pacific; the system, however, would not be able to justify its cost until late 1960s or early 1970s.

Various estimates of the cost of communications satellites have been made and considerable discrepancies became apparent between the figures quoted from various sources. Some of these estimates were very optimistic, while others appeared to be based on much sounder premises.

It has been suggested [7] that in global coverage the cost of establishing ground stations is a factor varying with altitude, since more stations would be needed to provide communications throughout the world when the satellites are in low orbits. The minimum cost for establishing the global coverage with vehicles randomly located will occur when circular polar orbits of about 6,000 miles are used, including a cost of approximately $32 million for ground stations and $93 million for the satellites. The minimum for controlled satellites occurs at a twenty-four-hour synchronous altitude, an estimated total of $70 million, including the four launches probably needed to set three satellites in orbit. An annual maintenance of $18 million to cover approximately two launches is required for the system.

Table 22 overleaf gives the estimated costs for establishing global coverage with repeater satellites in controlled orbits.

*

As matters stand at present, it is unlikely that *manned* orbitals or space vehicles will find commercial or civil applications in the course of the next two decades, with the possible exception of mapping and geodesic observatories and of more elaborate forms of communication stations. On the other hand, in the semi-ballistic régime area, some improved form of boost-glider of the Boeing *DynaSoar* type might be considered as a transport vehicle. It is doubtful, however, that the economics of hypersonic semi-ballistic craft could compare on an equal footing with the economics of conventional aircraft, including

[7] *Astronautics*, July 1961.

TABLE 22

Estimated costs of establishing global coverage with
repeater satellites in controlled orbits

Altitude in miles	Cost in $ million		
	Satellites	Ground installations	Total
4,000	180	45	225
6,000	120	33	153
8,000	90	30	120
10,000	75	30	105
12,000	62	30	92
14,000	52	30	82
16,000	45	30	75
18,000	40	30	70

the more expensive and technically-exacting variants such as the supersonic jetliner.

Nevertheless it is conceivable that hypersonic speeds will be justified in special cases, where short durations of travel take absolute precedence over cost—for example, express mail and VIP flights, say, from Vancouver to Auckland.[8] The term *antipodal* would be more accurate and put the boost-glider in its own category: the mere crossing of oceans is of lesser interest, since a fully-developed supersonic jetliner will shorten the duration to 2½ to 3½ hours, and a further increase of block speed will be offset by greatly inflated costs and seemingly inevitable delays on the ground, including archaic procedures such as passport inspection and customs.

A hypersonic antipodal service would be roughly of the same or possibly shorter duration, but the payload of a scaled-up derivative of the Boeing *DynaSoar* will be restricted and the fares only within reach of top-grade executives and government officials travelling on warrants eventually debited to the taxpayer.

Commercially speaking, special express mail and freight services might be considered, but pictorial transmission by

[8] Great circle distance: 7,060 miles.

cable or wireless—possibly via satellites—would offer very severe competition.

Whatever happens boost-glide transport will be feasible only if the initial research, development and prototype costs are met from military budgets or if defence hardware is used in the construction of the semi-ballistic flight vehicles. Thus, the most likely users will be the armed forces and the first hypersonic transports would, in fact, be military aircraft.

*

Finally, a few words about some of the indirect benefits to industry in general of research and development in the aerospace field. There is no need to emphasize the very exacting nature of the work involved in the construction, launching and operation of orbitals and space devices, further complicated by limitations of payloads carried which impose miniaturization techniques of a very advanced kind. Eventually such improvements will find applications on an expanding scale in surface transport, communications, controls, production machinery and even in what is loosely described as "consumer goods".

Aerospace communication and control equipment calls for light, long-duration power sources and the development of special auxiliary plants is one of the most important current requirements. Solar batteries and the direct conversion of nuclear heat into electricity are two typical areas of research which would benefit technologies other than aerospace proper.

The question of materials is of the utmost importance in all aerospace designs, particularly in vehicles intended for re-entry into the atmosphere. New alloys, ceramics and plastics are being reported constantly in the technical Press and here again "surface" technologies will benefit by the use of some of the simpler and cheaper forms of materials developed for aerospace.

The commercial advantages of a close collaboration between aerospace and other industries cannot be evaluated in figures—particularly at this early stage—but on a national scale the benefits of such co-operation would be very great, possibly resulting in the creation of entirely new types of products.

Conclusions

Some of the views expressed in the preceding chapters may sound bizarre; therefore it is necessary to emphasize once more the introductory remarks, namely, that *the aim of the present book is not an attempt at prophecy, but merely the exposition and logical extrapolation of certain basic hypotheses.*

Time will show whether the author's primary postulates were justified, but in the light of current events it seems unlikely that the technical forecasts will prove grossly inaccurate. The principal source of possible error lies in the political field, for instance a nuclear war occurring before aerospace science and technology provide the potential belligerents with new weapon systems which need not necessarily cause major devastation on the surface of the Earth. Another point is whether the conflict between West and East must be resolved in a radical fashion or that some form of genuine peaceful co-existence will be achieved. It can be said, however, that the sequence of events since 1945 makes the latter alternative distinctly improbable.

Soon after its inauguration the Kennedy Administration was reported to be against "summitry" and in favour of re-establishing contact with USSR through more conventional diplomatic channels. This has a bearing on matters discussed in the present essay: secret negotiations followed by public announcements of agreements prearranged after lengthy discussions seem more likely to preserve the precarious state of peace in the world. Moreover, this type of policy is consonant with the trends imposed by the development of new weapons, e.g. of military aerospace systems. It is easier and safer to hint at certain possible lines of action in the course of private talks than to make public statements on themes involving national prestige on a global scale. Alternatively, an overcautious and obscure communiqué may tempt the sensational Press to indulge in comments and guesses resulting in an increase of political tension. Secret diplomacy is more in keeping with the aerospace *élite arm*, particularly since the *deterrent credibility* of both USA and USSR tends to diminish with the growth of ballistic weapon inventories.

It is to be expected that discussions of various deterrent doctrines will continue for some time to come, but questions are now being asked and there is a distinct tendency to doubt the validity of some of the original fundamental assumptions. Critiques and comments have appeared in the Press; for instance, an article by General P. Gallois in a well-known French periodical.[1] It is clear that the value of the US nuclear deterrent *credibility factor*, as applied to Western Europe, is undergoing a marked change. It remains to be seen whether a strengthening of *conventional* forces will restore the position.

Even if there is an eventual reversal to strategic nuclear armaments, the spread and articulation of a NATO deterrent ballistic system would make the plan very complex. Moreover, it is not clear how the scheme would operate in an emergency; in other words, what agency or inter-Allied body is to be responsible for triggering off retaliation in the event of an attack against one of the NATO partners. This ultimate command problem is crucial and the French tendency towards an *independent deterrent* clearly shows that the idea of a "decision by committee" does not meet with universal and wholehearted approval.

In the submission of the present author a further devaluation of *credibility factors* and the growing complexity of air and ballistic deterrent systems will lead to a virtual political and strategic stalemate. So long as the decision to start a nuclear war remains in the hands of, say, three major Powers, a reasonable assessment of the situation can be made and forecasts hazarded for a few years ahead. The introduction of

[1] General P. Gallois: "Faut-il dénoncer le Pacte Atlantique?" *Réalités*, January 1961.

"deterrent committees" would bring in a number of unknowns, without necessarily increasing the *credibility factors* of the defence systems concerned.

It was also mentioned in Chapter I that the eventual emergence of "Minor Atomic Powers" would confuse the issue and increase the danger of a world conflagration. This must be realized by the leaders of the two opposing camps—USA and USSR—and, therefore, it is logical to expect a revival of interest in some form of nuclear disarmament agreement. It is improbable, however, that the chief protagonists will agree to the destruction of the whole or of a large portion of existing weapon stocks, but they might attempt to impose a qualified ban of all military nuclear experiments in the future. If such an agreement were arrived at it would be much more difficult for irresponsible minor Powers to build up atomic armaments and thus increase the risk of a global disaster.

The growing deterrent stalemate could also lead to an intensification of the Cold War: USA and USSR may be able to take bigger risks in local Cold War operations in Africa, South Eastern Asia and, say, the Carribean area.

It is not proposed to discuss here whether conventional forces and conventional armaments will be re-deployed on a larger scale. Historically it is improbable that high-efficiency atomic tactical weapons would be shelved and replaced by ordinary shells and bombs. Moreover, a race in conventional armaments would be against the interests of the Western Powers.

In addition to the difficulty of competing with USSR and its allies on a straightforward manpower basis, there remains the risk of a major conventional conflict finally bringing in tactical nuclear weapons. This is what is known as *escalation*, but there is no evidence to support the view that escalation need not necessarily lead to the use of major strategic nuclear armaments.

In fact, there is evidence to the contrary in a statement made by Mr. Khrushchev in the course of an interview with Mr. Walter Lippmann.[2] "We do not see any value in small tactical

[2] *The Observer* (London, April 23, 1961).

atomic weapons," he said; "if it comes to war, we shall use only the biggest weapons. The smaller ones are very expensive and they can decide nothing." This makes good sense, since the Russians have superiority in numbers and only stand to lose some of this advantage if tactical nuclear armaments were used in land battles. Thus they would be driven to *ultimate escalation*—the employment of strategic atomic weapons.

*

The conclusion suggested by the writer is that in the present state of the art of war—short of a global clash—there is no radical solution of the East-West conflict. Cold War operations are either inconclusive or—if escalation supervenes—the final issue could well be suicidal to both sides. Though there is now a school of thought professing that a major nuclear conflict need not end in utter and complete devastation, some of the assumptions made in the course of such dissertations make the conclusions unconvincing, in fact suspect. For instance, the originators of this "new" Douhet [3] concept appear to disregard the psychological aftermath of a major atomic war. Also, on the physical plane, the residual effects of nuclear explosions and fall-out are still uncertain: the latest Japanese statistics of long-term effects of Hiroshima and Nagasaki do not tally with the more optimistic American reports. Therefore it is hard to believe that responsible Governments would lightheartedly change their views on the probable results of an all-out nuclear conflict and foolishly assume that the victor would reap great political and economic benefits.

As a possible alternative to this static picture, both the US Administration and the USSR Government would continue to increase their aerospace programmes and budgets. The technological race would be intensified, but the fundamental trends may diverge in certain aspects. For instance, USSR might devote more time and money to interplanetary vehicles than

[3] Contemporary literature: *La Doctrine de Guerre du Général Douhet,* by Colonel P. Vauthier, Editions Berger-Levrault, Paris, 1935.

USA; in practice this would mean that the Russians would make an all-out effort to achieve a series of further "firsts", including a soft landing on the Moon. This, however, does not mean they would neglect orbital armaments.

USA is more likely to concentrate on aerospace work, communication and reconnaissance satellites being the clearest current items of the programme. No doubt more advanced projects will be pursued, such as NABS (Nuclear-Armed Bombardment Satellites) and anti-orbital weapons, but they will probably be played down at public relations level to avoid accusations of aggressive intentions in orbital space. Nevertheless, whatever steps are taken by the Kennedy Administration to minimize friction with USSR, the day must come when the Soviets will be compelled to take *official notice* of American reconnaissance, mapping and surveillance satellites overflying their territory. Thus another *U-2* controversy is to be expected, arising out of some incident in orbital space; such an incident might take the form of an interception of an American orbiter by a Russian anti-orbital device.

The interception of a satellite by an anti-orbital will be an historical date—the first combat in space. Logically this must be followed by a further growth and improvement of aerospace armaments which would eventually lead to open "robot warfare" between two Powers striving to achieve *aerospace supremacy*.

At the risk of repetition, it must be emphasized once more that an eventual full-scale orbital war might be the only humane solution of the apparently insoluble East-West ideological and political opposition. If the fundamental hypotheses on which the present book is based prove to be correct, the conflict would be thus resolved without major physical repercussions on the surface of the Earth.

The implications of these new possibilities in the realm of Grand Strategy are such that the Western European nations cannot afford to ignore the rapid and, in a way, menacing development of aerospace science and technology. Unless it is assumed that the defence of the whole of the Western hemisphere is to be wholly dependent upon USA, the non-American

NATO members must at least make the initial effort of a full and unbiased evaluation of aerospace from the political, military, industrial and commercial points of view.

The penalty for inaction and lack of interest will be the eventual devaluation of the political and strategic status of Western European nations—including Britain. Uninformed scepticism and an attitude of *laissez faire* are among the surest ways of reducing highly civilized and virile peoples to the level of political helots—or worse, to that of demographic material.

APPENDIX I

TABLE 23

Orbitals and probes successfully launched up to July 1, 1961

Index	Name	Dates		Apogee, (statute miles)	Perigee, (statute miles)	Period, (min)	Remarks
		Launch	Decay				
1957 Alpha	Sputnik 1 (USSR)	4/10/57	Jan. '58	—	—	—	
1957 Beta	Sputnik 2 (USSR)	3/11/57	14/4/58	—	—	—	
1958 Alpha	Explorer 1 (USA)	1/2/58		1,120	217	106.6	
1958 Beta	Vanguard 1 (USA)	17/3/58		2,455	404	133.9	Transmitting
1958 Gamma	Explorer 3 (USA)	26/3/58	28/6/58	—	—	—	
1958 Delta	Sputnik 3 (USSR)	15/5/58	6/4/60	—	—	—	
1958 Epsilon	Explorer 4 (USA)	26/7/58	23/10/59	—	—	—	
1958 Zeta	Atlas (USA)	18/12/58	21/1/59	—	—	—	
1958 Eta	Pioneer 1 (USA)	11/10/58	12/10/58	—	—	—	
1958 Theta	Pioneer 3 (USA)	6/12/58	7/12/58	—	—	—	
1959 Alpha	Vanguard 2 (USA)	17/2/59		2,052	343	125.4	
1959 Beta	Discoverer 1 (USA)	28/2/59	Mar. '59	—	—	—	
1959 Gamma	Discoverer 2 (USA)	13/4/59	26/4/59				
1959 Delta	Explorer 4 (USA)	7/8/59		Position uncertain			
1959 Epsilon 1	Discoverer 5 (USA)	13/8/59	28/9/59	—	—	—	
1959 Epsilon 2	Capsule	13/8/59	11/2/61	—	—	—	

Index	Name	Dates		Apogee, (statute miles)	Perigee, (statute miles)	Period, (min)	Remarks
		Launch	Decay				
1959 Zeta	Discoverer 6 (USA)	19/8/59	20/10/59	—	—	—	
1959 Eta	Vanguard 3 (USA)	18/9/59		2,318	322	129.8	
1959 Mu	Lunik 1 (USSR)	2/1/59		extra-terrestrial orbit			
1959 Nu	Pioneer 4 (USA)	3/3/59		extra-terrestrial orbit			
1959 Theta	Lunik 3 (USSR)	4/10/59	Apr. '60				
1959 Iota	Explorer 7 (USA)	13/10/59		699	344	101.1	Transmitting
1959 Kappa	Discoverer 7 (USA)	7/11/59	26/11/59				
1959 Lambda	Discoverer 8 (USA)	20/11/59	8/3/60	—	—	—	Moon impact
1959 Xi	Lunik 2 (USSR)	12/9/59	13/9/59	extra-terrestrial orbit			
1960 Alpha	Pioneer 5 (USA)	11/3/60					
1960 Beta	Tiros 1 (USA)	1/4/60		467	429	99.1	Transmitting
1960 Gamma	Transit 1B (USA)	13/4/60		417	229	95	
1960 Delta	Discoverer 11 (USA)	15/4/60	26/4/60	—	—	—	
1960 Epsilon	Sputnik 4 (USSR)	15/5/60		322	175	92.6	
1960 Zeta	Midas 2 (USA)	24/5/60		315	297	94.3	
1960 Eta 1	Transit 2A (USA)	22/6/60		649	389	101.6	
1960 Eta 2	Greb (USA)	22/6/60		657	381	101.6	Transmitting
1960 Theta	Discoverer 13 (USA)	10/8/60	14/11/60	—	—	—	
ditto	Capsule	10/8/60	11/8/60	—	—	—	Re-entry and recovery
1960 Iota	Echo 1 (USA)	12/8/60		994	934	117	

Index	Name	Dates Launch	Dates Decay	Apogee, (statute miles)	Perigee, (statute miles)	Period, (min)	Remarks
1960 Kappa ·	Discoverer 14 (USA)	18/8/60	16/9/60	—	—	—	Re-entry and recovery
ditto ·	Capsule	18/8/60	19/8/60	—	—	—	Re-entry and recovery
1960 Lambda ·	Sputnik 5 (USSR)	19/8/60	20/8/60	—	—	—	
1960 Mu ·	Discoverer 15 (USA)	13/9/60	18/10/60	—	—	—	
ditto ·	Capsule	13/9/60	15/9/60	—	—	—	Transmitting
1960 Mu I ·	Courier 1B (USA)	4/10/60	—	750	604	106.9	
1960 Xi I ·	Explorer 8 (USA)	3/11/60	—	1,412	262	112.6	
1960 Omicron ·	Discoverer 17 (USA)	12/11/60	29/12/60	—	—	—	Re-entry and recovery
ditto ·	Capsule	12/11/60	14/11/60	—	—	—	Transmitting
1960 Pi I ·	Tiros 2 (USA)	23/11/60	—	461	373	98.2	
1960 Rho ·	Sputnik 4 (USSR)	1/12/60	2/12/60	—	—	—	
1960 Sigma ·	Discoverer 18 (USA)	7/12/60	2/4/61	—	—	—	Re-entry and recovery
ditto ·	Capsule	7/12/60	10/12/61	—	—	—	
1960 Tau ·	Discoverer 19 (USA)	20/12/60	23/1/61	—	—	—	
1961 Alpha ·	Samos 2 (USA)	31/1/61	—	342	295	94.9	
1961 Beta ·	Sputnik 7 (USSR)	4/2/61	26/2/61	—	—	—	
1961 Gamma I ·	Venus Probe (USSR)	12/2/61	—	extra-terrestrial orbit			
1961 Gamma 3 ·	Sputnik 8 (USSR)	12/2/61	25/2/61	—	—	—	
1961 Delta ·	Explorer 9 (USA)	16/2/61	—	1,580	430	118.2	
1961 Epsilon ·	Discoverer 20 (USA)	17/2/61	—	444	176	94.7	

Index	Name	Dates		Apogee, (statute miles)	Perigee, (statute miles)	Period, (min)	Remarks
		Launch	Decay				
1961 Zeta .	Discoverer 21 (USA)	18/2/61	30/3/61	572	154	96.6	
1961 Eta .	Transit 3B (USA)	22/2/61	30/3/61	—	—	—	
ditto .	Lofti (USA)	22/2/61	9/3/61	—	—	—	Re-entry and recovery
1961 Theta	Sputnik 9 (USSR)	9/3/61		Position uncertain			Re-entry and recovery
1961 Kappa	Explorer 10 (USA)	25/3/61					
1961 Iota .	Sputnik 10 (USSR)	25/3/61	25/3/61				Re-entry and recovery
1961 Lambda	Discoverer 23 (USA)	8/4/61		372	183	93.6	
ditto .	Capsule	8/4/61		828	126	100.3	
1961 Mu .	Vostok 1 (USSR)	12/4/61	12/4/61	—	—	—	Manned re-entry
1961 Nu .	Explorer 11 (USA)	27/4/61		1,107	302	107.9	Transmitting
1961 Xi .	Discoverer 25 (USA)	16/6/61	18/6/61	250	139	90.8	
ditto .	Capsule	16/6/61		—	—	—	Re-entry and recovery
1961 Omicron .	Transit 4A (USA)	28/6/61		628	557	104	Transmitting
ditto .	Greb 3	28/6/61		628	557	104	
ditto .	Injun	28/6/61		628	557	104	

141

Sources: NASA Operations Control Centre, North American Air Defense Command and Smithsonian Astrophysical Observatory (*Aviation Week and Space Technology*, August 7, 1961).

APPENDIX II

KILL PROBABILITIES OF BALLISTIC WEAPONS
(see p. 9)

Let k denote probability of first shot kill (as fraction of unity):

$$k = 1 - (0.5)^{R^2/C^2}$$

where R = radius of effect in nautical miles,
$\quad\quad C$ = circular probable error (CEP) in nautical miles.

Also,
$$R = \frac{0.46 \sqrt[3]{Y}}{\sqrt[3\cdot1]{p}}$$

where Y = yield in kilotons,
$\quad\quad p$ = overpressure in p.s.i.
$\quad\quad\quad$ (p for attack of underground missile sites = 100 p.s.i.;
$\quad\quad\quad$ p for attack of cities = 5–10 p.s.i.).

Let S denote fraction of force expected to survive:

$$S = (1 - k)^{rE/M}$$

where r = reliability of attacking missiles (as fraction of unity),
$\quad\quad E$ = number of attacking missiles,
$\quad\quad M$ = number of missiles under attack.

Bibliography

ERIC BURGESS: *Long-Range Ballistic Missiles*. Chapman and Hall, London, 1961.

W. R. DORNBERGER: *V-2*. Viking, New York, 1954.

General PIERRE GALLOIS: *Stratégie de l'Age Nucléaire*. Calmann-Levy, Paris, 1960. *The Balance of Terror*. Houghton Mifflin Company, Boston, and the Riverside Press, Cambridge, Mass., 1961.

K. W. GATLAND: *Development of the Guided Missile*. Second Edition, Iliffe, London, 1954 *and* Philosophical Library, New York, 1954.

H. KAHN: *On Thermonuclear War*. Princeton University, 1960.

ASHER LEE: *The Soviet Air Force*. Duckworth, London, 1961.

G. POKROVSKY: *Science and Technology in Contemporary War*. Atlantic Books (USA), and Stevens and Sons (London).

M. W. ROSEN: *The Viking Rocket Story*. Faber and Faber, London, 1956.

ARI SHTERNFELD: *Soviet Space Science*. Basic Books, New York, 1959.

The Effects of Nuclear Weapons. US Atomic Energy Commission, 1952.

Industry and Space. Hawker Siddeley Aviation, Ltd., London, and SEREB, Paris, private publication, 1961.

Index

144

CPSIA information can be obtained
at www.ICGtesting.com
Printed in the USA
BVOW06s1807140517
484114BV00008B/81/P